DIVERSITY IN FAMILY LIFE

Gender, relationships and social change

Elisabetta Ruspini

First published in Great Britain in 2013 by

Policy Press
University of Bristol
Fourth Floor
Beacon House
Queen's Road
Bristol BS8 1QU
UK
Tel +44 (0)117 331 4054
Fax +44 (0)117 331 4093
e-mail tpp-info@bristol.ac.uk
www.policypress.co.uk

North American office:
Policy Press
c/o The University of Chicago Press
1427 East 60th Street
Chicago, IL 60637, USA
t: +1 773 702 7700
f: +1 773 702 9756
e:sales@press.uchicago.edu
www.press.uchicago.edu

British Library Cataloguing in Publication Data
A catalogue record for this book is available from the British Library.

Library of Congress Cataloging-in-Publication Data
A catalog record for this book has been requested.

ISBN 978 1 44730 093 9 hardcover

Cover design by Policy Press.
Front cover: image kindly supplied by www.alamy.com
Printed and bound in Great Britain by TJ International, Padstow
Policy Press uses environmentally responsible print partners

MIX
Paper from
responsible sources
FSC
www.fsc.org
FSC° C013056

This book is dedicated to my Millennial children: Maddalena Emma and Andrea Emanuele.

Contents

Acknowledgements

I wish to deeply acknowledge the very precious help provided by Naomi Rosenthal, whose comments and suggestions helped to review the first version of the book.

INTRODUCTION

Gender, family and social change: from modernity to the Millennial generation

This volume provides a road map through the challenges of family diversity and family change in Western societies. Family forms, what it means to be a member of a family and the expectations people have of family relationships vary with time and space. As we will shortly see, today, marriage and family relationships are formed and maintained in an environment of greater choice in how women and men can live their lives than has been possible for past generations. Following Beck (1992), choices are made in a world that no longer has universal certainties, risks and fixed models of life.

Changing **gender identities**[1] – gender identity may be defined as a person's inner sense of being a woman or a man, or another **gender** – have had a direct impact on the processes of family formation and models of motherhood and fatherhood in the Western experience. Obviously, gender identities and **gender roles** provide much of the organising structure in family life (Barnard and Martell, 1995; Parke, 1995), and, we would argue, changes in gender identities and in **gender relations** are at the root of family and **social change** (Demo et al, 2000; Hall, 2000; Erera, 2002; Sullivan, 2006; Klett-Davies, 2007; Gabb, 2008; Lamanna and Riedmann, 2009; Kapella et al, 2010; Woodward, 2011).

In particular, we notice a move towards more individualised and flexible decision-making processes, distant from the formal frameworks that used to shape women's and men's decisions in matters of relationships and family life. In fact, it is possible to identify many diverse family structures today, such as one-parent families, unmarried couples with children, Lesbian, Gay, Bisexual, Transsexual, Transgender, Intersex and **Queer** (LGBTTIQ) families, divorced families, reconstructed families, mixed families, couples where the two partners live in separated domiciles, and asexual and childfree couples (see, eg, Demo et al, 2000; Beck-Gernsheim, 2002; Baca Zinn et al, 2010).

These new living arrangements are the communes of the 21st century, the century inhabited by the Millennial generation (also 'Digital' or 'Net' generation). The Millennials are the newest generation, a group of young people whose birth years range from 1980 to 1982 onwards.[2]

Millennials are mostly the children of **Baby Boomers** or **Generation Xers**. In recent years, the Millennial generation has emerged as a powerful political and social force. The Millennial generation has been defined as one that is competent, qualified, technological and in search of a new form of citizenship (Howe and Strauss, 2000; Balduzzi and Rosina, 2009; Benckendorff et al, 2010; Rainer and Rainer, 2011; Taylor and Keeter, 2010). They are politically and socially independent, and they are thus spearheading a period of sweeping change around the world (Greenberg and Weber, 2008). This is for various reasons.

First, they are the most ethnically and racially diverse cohort of youth in history. In the US, among those aged 13 to 29, 18.5% are Hispanic, 14.2% are black, 4.3% are Asian, 3.2% are mixed race or other and 59.8%, a record low, are white (Keeter and Taylor, 2009). Millennials are thus starting out as the most politically progressive age group in modern history.[3] Second, they feel empowered, they have a sense of security and they are optimistic about the future. Unlike generations that came before them (Baby Boomers and Generation Xers), these children are not left to make key decisions on their own; the parents are involved in their daily lives. Their parents helped them plan their achievements, took part in their activities and showed strong beliefs about their children's abilities. Third, they are extremely independent because of individual and family change (divorced families, 'new' family forms, lone parenting, etc) and the revolution of advanced Internet technologies. The Millennials grew up with Web 2.0 technologies[4] and thrive in a multimedia, highly communicative environment. Learning online is 'natural' to them – as much as retrieving and creatively creating information on the internet, blogging, communicating on cell phones, downloading files to iPods and instant messaging.[5] Following Keeter and Taylor (2009), they are the first generation in human history to regard behaviours like tweeting and texting, along with websites like Facebook, YouTube, Google and Wikipedia, not as astonishing innovations of the digital era, but as everyday parts of their social lives and their search for understanding. The oldest members of this generation are now entering the workforce. At the same time, the Baby Boom generation is retiring at a much older age than members of previous generations. This may bring about intergenerational conflicts, as well as uncertainty about what the future of workforce will be.[6]

A book by Greenberg and Weber (2008), which explores the values, dreams and potential of the Millennial generation, shows that they (and their supporters from other generations) are poised to change the world for the better, and lays out a powerful plan for progressive change that today's youth is ready to implement. The book presents the results of a major research study into the characteristics of the Millennial generation, including an in-depth survey of 2,000 individuals and a series of 12 geographically and demographically diverse focus groups. A second book – based on 1,200 interviews – by Rainer and Rainer (2011) sheds lights on the relationship between the Millennial generation, **intimacy**, marriage and family formation. When Millennials were asked about parental involvement, 89% responded that they received guidance and advice from their parents. It turned out that the Baby Boomers are helping Millennials make decisions about work and life. While previous generations might have rejected such advice, 87% of Millennials view their parents as a positive source of influence. When it comes to marriage, Millennials are optimistic about it even though they grew up in a world where divorce was common. It is also worth noting that Millennials are marrying much later than any generation that had preceded them. They also view marriage differently from their parents, in part because of the political battles concerning same-sex marriage and the definition of marriage. In the survey, they were asked to respond to the following statement: 'I see nothing wrong with two people of the same gender getting married'. Six in 10 agree with the statement (40% strongly agreed, 21% agreed somewhat). In other words, a significant majority of Millennials see nothing wrong with same-sex marriage.

It is also likely that the pluralisation of family forms and arrangements will further increase; following some evidence (Taylor and Keeter, 2010; Rainer and Rainer, 2011; Stanton and Hess, 2012), Millennials are continuing the prior generational trend of being increasingly in favour of new family forms, but by a higher margin. The Millennials are more tolerant than adults in other generations of a wide range of 'non-traditional' behaviours related to marriage and parenting. These young people are negotiating their love and sexual relationships in an increasingly fluid environment (Giddens, 1992).

The impact of technology on marriage, family life and family diversity is also significant. Technology is probably the feature that has changed the most dramatically since the modern period. Many of the changes discussed earlier are being accelerated by the emergence of information and communication technologies (ICTs). Because of the new technologies, new forms of **culture** are emerging (Venkatesh et al, 1995). As said, the Millennial generation has grown up with the internet, cell phones and social media. It is easier than ever to call on a cell phone or send a text to other members of one's extended family. Posting pictures on Facebook allows family members to immediately see what is happening to their children and grandchildren. Thus,

Millennials are introducing their families to a variety of ways to stay connected (Anderson, 2011).

Family, family change, modernity

The family has never been a fixed entity. As Mintz and Kellogg (1988, p xiv) note, although the family is seen as a social institution most resistant to change, it is, in fact, as deeply embedded in the historical process as any other institution. The claim that it is essentially a conservative institution, an island of stability, is largely an illusion. Families have changed dramatically over time due to economic, demographic, cultural and political factors. In this view, families should not be considered as 'building blocks of societies', but, rather, as products of social forces within societies (Baca Zinn et al, 2010).

For our purposes, family change should be viewed in the context of all the other changes that have occurred under what has, alternately, been called 'second', 'late', 'high', 'new', or 'post-'modernity (see, eg, Lyotard, 1979; Giddens, 1990, 1991; Bauman, 1992; Beck, 1992; Beck and Beck-Gernsheim, 1995; Browning et al, 2000; Eisenstadt, 2005; Taylor-Gooby, 2005; Beck and Grande, 2010). As we will see later on, in social theory, the debate is still open as to whether the process of modernity is complete, whether we have entered into a second, late or mature form of modernity, or whether we have progressed into and beyond a process of post-modernity.

The transition from modernity to contemporary[7] modernity has been demarcated by radical transitions in the last few decades – including: globalisation; sectoral deindustrialisation; the de-standardisation and increasing precariousness of labour; rising education levels; and recurrent economic and political crises – which have been accompanied by a restructuring of intergenerational relations and the transformation of gender identities and family models. For example, as Irving (2008) argues, the shift from industrial modernity to late or post-modernity allows us to reconsider gendered notions of 'work' and 'care' (see also Robinson and Hockey, 2011). Gendered work relations in the global North are also in transition in response to social and economic change, facilitating a shift from the traditional male breadwinner model of family life to, as yet, unestablished models.

However, the terms 'late', 'second' or 'post-'modernity should not mean, as we will shortly see, that the past is of no importance in the structures of family life. The interplay between past, present and future is always relevant and should not be taken for granted. For example, as Taylor-Gooby (2005) notes, it is important to be clear that social change does not imply that risks and uncertainties are any more salient than they were at the height of the modern period – when morbidity and mortality rates were higher, living standards lower and (for much of the 20th century) the dangers to the citizens of the developed world from economic instability and war much greater. The claim here is rather that a *cultural* shift in the institution of the family is now well underway.

Social change has favoured a drawing closer of male and female life courses, both from the structural point of view (an increase in women's employment and schooling, delayed entry into adult life, a shared and lesser inclination for marriage and procreation, and the assumption by women of responsibilities that previously belonged exclusively to men, etc) and in the way in which life courses are desired, planned, constructed and redefined by individuals themselves. However, many people still plan their lives on the assumption that the traditional patterns of relationship will endure (Williams, 2004; Oinonen, 2008), and most social care continues to be provided domestically by women kin (Crompton, 1997). Moreover, if the deep divisions between male and female roles – which seem to have been deeply embedded in the Western past – persist, the intense transformations that have affected **life courses** must be accommodated. But let us proceed one step at a time.

Scholars agree that **social change** accelerated[8] with the transition to modernity (Haferkamp and Smelser, 1992), beginning (in Western Europe) in the late 17th century and ending by the second half of the 20th century. A very long and complex historical phase, it can be subdivided into smaller phases (see, eg, Harvey, 1989; Jameson, 1991). Modernity typically refers to a post-traditional, post-medieval historical period, one marked by the move from feudalism (or agrarianism) towards capitalism, industrialisation, urbanisation, rationalisation, a standardised education system, a centralised bureaucratic government, the pervasive use of technology, the nation-state and its institutions, and forms of social control.

Modernity represents a stage in the development of knowledge, normatively linked to a positive image of progress. According to Bauman (1992), it has constituted a movement with a *specific* direction, a direction driven by industrialisation, standardisation and rationalisation. However, modernity cannot be equated with capitalism because capitalism is only *one* type of modernity.

Modernity also involves the liberation and increasing autonomy of associations of action in almost all societal areas (Haferkamp and Smelser, 1992). Proponents of secularisation theory, such as Peter L. Berger (1999), Thomas Luckmann (1967) and Bryan Wilson (1982), established a strong connection between the beginning of modernity and the decline of traditional forms of religious life.

Gender relations were, according to most scholars, directly affected by the transition to modernity. Arguably, romantic love (as the ideal basis for contractual marriage, which is a relatively recent phenomenon in human history) could be seen as one of the side effects of the dissolution of feudal, peasant society and the emergence of the market principles of capitalism, increasing individualism and individual property. As Macfarlane (1987) writes, love between men and women as the basis of marriage is a central feature of modern industrial societies:

> Intuitively there seems to be something plausible in the idea that the individualism of love marriage is linked to the individualism of modern society and of the 'free' person operating within a monetized, market, capitalistic system where he, or she, has individual property in his or her own body.

Love, or deep affection between members of the opposite sex, is certainly not unknown before modernity and/or outside modern industrial societies (see, eg, Westermarck, 1921; Rousseau and Rosenthal, 1998; Murray, 2001). However, if we distinguish between love outside and within marriage, there is a certain peculiarity of the Western pattern. Following Macfarlane (1987), what seems peculiar is the fact that the decision to marry should be based on the premise that love and marriage are indistinguishably united.

Particularly in peasant societies, marriage was largely based on arrangements by kin or other wider groups and personal feelings were not of concern: marriage was too important a matter to be left to the individuals concerned (ie choices dependent on attraction, feelings, romanticism, etc).

However, alongside progress and development, modernity is not without its contrasts and tensions (Giddens, 1990; Bauman, 1992). Modernity consists of cultural, economic and social patterns linked to industrialisation; and the industrialisation process required strong social, economic, political and cultural support. It may well have been the cultural and social gender dichotomy – historically constructed around male and female biological features – that ensured the conditions for the development and survival of industrial society (Zemon Davis et al, 1993; Scott, 1995; Fraisse et al, 2000; Bock, 2009).

In the transition to industrialism, families lost many of their production functions. In the pre-industrial period, the family was the unit of production: the family worked together as a unit and was self-sufficient (see, eg, Tilly and Scott, 1987; Mintz and Kellogg, 1998; Janssens 2002). Family life was characterised by an interweaving of the husband's and wife's involvement with domestic life and with a productive work life: the pre-industrial family economy expected all its members, including women, to work in the interest of the family.

With the Industrial Revolution, large-scale production replaced home manufacturing and family members had to work outside the home to support their families. The Industrial Revolution also led to a new wave of urbanisation. The increasing number of factories created an intense need for labour, inducing people in rural areas to move to the city, and also drawing immigrants from, for example, Europe to the US or from Southern European to Northern European countries. Concentration in urban and industrial areas lent a different dynamic to cities, changing them both socially and physically. Legislation was introduced restricting employment hours for women and children, thus restricting women's employment opportunities. As a result, in the ideal family, husbands and wives were to operate in separate spheres of activity, both in spatial and in temporal terms. The husband was to be the 'breadwinner' by working outside the home, while the wife was to stay in the household in order to care for the family (see, eg, Tilly and Scott, 1987; Giles, 2004; Hoffman, 2004). That arrangement both supported **social reproduction** and functioned to reproduce the labour force.

As Max Weber (1946) pointed out, love and sexual desire, being one of the strongest non-rational factors in human life and one of the strongest potential menaces to the individual's rational pursuit of economic ends, had to be placed under strong control, particularly in the ideology of capitalism (Watt, 1957, p 67; Cipolla, 1996). Love, eroticism and **sexuality** were domesticated, and the forces were channelled and controlled: love became one of the central dynamic elements in the capitalist system (Macfarlane, 1987). We may, for example, think of the idealisation of marriage, of the emphasis on the spiritual values of the marriage relationship, and of the Puritanism attitude that was particularly vigorous in enforcing the sinfulness of all sexual activities outside marriage (Watt, 1957, p 156). Of course, the institution of marriage has always been enveloped in a series of restrictions. From age, to race, to social status, to consanguinity, to gender, restrictions have everywhere imbricated marital relations in order to protect children and kin, and property arrangements, to pass on desired characteristics, to maintain cultural values or because of prejudice and fear.[9] As Berger and Kellner (1964) wrote, marriage might be described as a 'dramatic act' in which two strangers come together and redefine themselves (Hackstaff, 1999). Yet, the major purpose of marriage (as an institution) has not only been to normalise and to control, but also to satisfy the multiple needs of the individuals concerned. Thus, it is a compromise between cultural and social necessities, on the one hand, and psychological, emotional and sexual needs, on the other.

Modernity (especially in the last phases of this long historical era) was thus characterised by idealised, standardised life courses, a strong gender polarisation, and families with a single, stable wage-earner, where the salary of the male head of the family functioned as a family wage. The rigid conception of the man–woman relation was expressed through a delimiting of ways of being, characters and behaviours, as well as roles. This often created a very burdensome constraint, for both sexes: a constraint that was socially guaranteed and controlled.

A well-known example of the emphasis on gender polarisation includes major theories of family life developed, for example, by Talcott Parsons (1943, 1954) and Becker (1981). For many years, Talcott Parsons was the best-known sociologist in the US, and, indeed, one of the best-known in the world. He produced a general theoretical system for the analysis of society that came to be called 'structural functionalism'. Parsons clearly theorised the separation of roles between women and men and the differentiation of the sexual roles in the family. Mother and father are representatives and bearers, for their children, of two distinct, complementary codes. The husband-father is the instrumental leader, assigned with the management of social relations and the financial support of the family and its members; he is the parent who indicates limits and duties, who exercises authority and who promotes the interiorisation of the rules of social living. The wife-mother, instead, has the role of expressive leadership centred on internal relations within the family and its affective function: she is the parent with the task of ensuring the immediate satisfaction of children's needs, tending to their emotional and physical needs. For structural functionalists, the biological-sexual difference essentially corresponds to a difference in aptitude that reserves different specific scopes to men and women, being functional to the maintenance of order and equilibrium in society. And the family is interpreted as a functional necessity, because without it, the human species would die out. Many **gender stereotypes** are based upon a structural functionalist argument that men and women have biologically and socially evolved to be suited to different tasks, with the men as breadwinners and the women as carers.

Motherhood is intimately connected to strong assumptions about mothers and fathers, women and men, families in general, and society at large. As Badinter (1981) notes, modern motherhood undermines the status of women – attachment parenting, co-sleeping, baby-wearing and especially breast-feeding, these hallmarks have succeeded in tethering women to the home and family to an extent not seen since the 1950s. Feminist authors such as Lorber (2000) argue for the 'degendering' of society. For Lorber, the division of people into two unequally valued categories underpins gender inequality. Lorber (2000) argues for moving towards a non-gendered social order, based on equality, without gender categorisation.

Many other examples testify to the cultural, social, legislative and political control over gender polarisation, sexual activity and sexual orientation. In Russia, in the years following the Russian Revolution, many attempts were made to define and control sexual behaviour. In her book, Frances Lee Bernstein (2007) examines the Soviet 'sexual enlightenment', a programme of popular health and lifestyle advice intended to establish a model of sexual conduct for the men and women who would build socialism.

A second example is the 20-year period of Fascist rule (1922–43). The nationalistic and imperialist Fascist agenda took a strong pro-natalist position. The regime associated motherhood, children, family and virility with maintaining national greatness (Di Nicola, 1983; De Grazia, 1992; Gori, 1999; Benadusi, 2012). The battle for births took place during the interwar years of 1925–38 (Forcucci, 2010). The demographic campaign promoted fertility, especially within the working class, by increasing welfare benefits, legislating for tax breaks, making better health care available and awarding public medals and recognition to those women who produced more than the state's target of five children per family. Moreover, promiscuous male sexuality, like female eroticism, was to be exorcised and normalised to remove any danger that might emerge from failure to marry, homosexuality or any impulse for emancipation. Thus, women (destined to become mothers and wives) were encaged in a public cult of domesticity, and men (as heads of families) were committed to sowing their seed. The close link between virility and offspring is expressed by Mussolini's tax on 'unjustified' celibacy (or tax on bachelors) of 1926 that condemned infertile men (priests, men certified as infirm and servicemen on active duty were exempted). The measure had a typically homophobic dimension (De Grazia, 1992, pp 69–70). It also reflects the efforts made by 20th-century masculinity to defend the traditional gender order from the threats of modernisation and the growing self-promotion of women (Mosse, 1998).

A third example refers to Spain. The process towards family diversity and acceptance of homosexuality was suddenly interrupted by the Spanish Civil War and Franco's regime, which precipitated a strong repression of the LGBTTIQ community in Spain. Homosexuality was highly illegal under Franco's dictatorship, with laws against homosexual activity vigorously enforced and gays being imprisoned and often tortured in large numbers. The 1954 reform of the 1933 *Ley de vagos y maleantes* (Vagrancy Act) declared homosexuality illegal. Franco's dictatorship lasted from 1939 to his death in November 1975.

A final, illuminating example. The Catholic Church rejects abortion, contraception and sterilisation, and affirms that the primary end of marriage is the procreation and education of a new life. It opposes same-sex relationships/marriages: however, it teaches that homosexual persons deserve respect, justice and pastoral care. Following the *Congregatio pro Istitutione Catholica* (Congregation for Catholic Education) (CIC, 1983), homosexual people might benefit from medical–psychological assistance. Such assistance must also come from persons attentive to and respectful of the teachings of the Church. Very recently (June 2003), the *Congregatio pro Doctrina Fidei* (Congregation for the Doctrine of the Faith; CDF) set forth the inalienable characteristics of marriage. The CDF firmly asserts that homosexual unions are not in any way similar to God's plan for marriage and the family. It adds that where homosexual unions have been legally recognised by civil authorities, 'clear and emphatic opposition' is the duty of every Catholic. The CDF (2003) affirms:

> There are absolutely no grounds for considering homosexual unions to be in any way similar or even remotely analogous to God's plan for marriage and family. Marriage is holy, while homosexual acts go against the natural moral law. Homosexual acts close the sexual act to the gift of life. They do not proceed from a genuine affective and sexual complementarity. Under no circumstances can they be approved.

Vatican City does not have any civil rights provisions that include sexual orientation or gender identity.[10]

Family, family change, contemporary modernities

Let us now take one step forward. Social change generated by what has been called the transition from modernity to late or post-modernity in the second half of the 20th century has been described by many scholars as accelerated, producing altered social structures in a number of different and unexpected directions. Since about the early 1970s, we are supposed to have been living in a new historical epoch. As said earlier, this epoch has been defined in various ways (Wood, 1996). Late, second, high, new and post-modernity are different terms used to describe the condition of today's societies.

Conceptualising the contemporary condition as a continuation or development of modernity, rather than as a distinct new state, that is, post-modernity, the concept of 'late modernity' proposes that contemporary societies are a clear continuation of modern institutional transitions and cultural developments.[11] Some accounts emphasise cultural changes ('reflexive society', 'digital age', 'information age'), while others focus more on economic transformations, changes in production and marketing, or in corporate and financial organisation ('late capitalism', 'post-Fordism', 'globalisation', etc). Late modernity is thus a characterisation of the type of social organisation that has been produced by modernisation, a product of political and industrial revolution.

Post-modernity is a term generally used to describe the social, cultural, economic and political characteristics of the society that is said to exist *after* modernity. Sociologists such as Ulrich Beck, Zygmunt Bauman and Anthony Giddens (Giddens, 1990, 1991; Bauman, 1992; Beck, 1992; Beck and Beck-Gernsheim, 1995) criticise adherents of post-modernity that presume the ending of the modernisation process and the dawning of a new era. Rather, contemporary modernity, they argue, involves a continuation or even a radicalisation of the modernisation process.

Postmodernism emerged in academic studies in the mid-1980s. Following Jameson (1991), postmodernism emerged as a reaction against the established forms of older modernism, a worldview that emphasises the existence of different concepts of reality, rather than one 'correct' or 'true'. Whereas modernism emphasised a trust in the empirical scientific method, and a distrust and lack of faith in ideologies and religious beliefs that could not be tested using scientific methods, postmodernism emphasises that a particular reality is a social construction by a specific group, community or class of persons. Another feature of postmodernism is the effacement in it of some key boundaries or separations, most notably, the erosion of the older distinction between high culture and so-called mass or popular culture (Jameson, 1991).

Thus, contemporary modernity is demarcated from modernity by a broad reversal in cultural presuppositions and norms. As Jean-François

Lyotard (1979) and Anthony Giddens (1991) note, this era is characterised by: an increasing scepticism and incredulity towards meta-narratives[12]; less or no worry about the precedents set by previous generations; diversity; a multiplicity of communities of meaning; and an increase in the available information and the reflexive application of this information. In this view, categories such as class and social status, **gender roles**, and family are supposed to have become increasingly fragile and replaced with new models, demands and challenges. As far as gender is concerned, the period of modernist dichotomies – that is, gender polarisation – is coming to an end as we begin to enter the late or post-modern era.

Where classic modernity was characterised by class-based societies that shaped people's lives as destiny, in contemporary modernity, men and women are much freer to shape their own destinies (Touraine, 2005). Following the cultural revolution of the late 1960s and 1970s (which was itself fuelled by a post-war prosperity that allowed people to give greater attention to non-material concerns), late modernity played a key role in reconfiguring views of marriage and family life. Prior to the late 1960s, men and women were more likely to look at marriage and family through the prisms of duty, obligation and sacrifice: financial dependence and societal pressure led to couples remaining together despite unhappiness in the relationship. Cherlin (2007) also suggests that especially after the 1960s, marriage came to be regarded as a means for self-development and emotional expression, rather than a vehicle for satisfaction in performing traditional roles of spouse and parent.

Late modern society is characterised by a crucial process, called *reflexive modernisation* (Beck and Beck-Gernsheim, 2001). It is essentially an acceleration and radicalisation of the development of core institutional features of modern society. Reflexive modernisation throws all basic social principles into flux in that it undermines modern society as modernisation has undermined the traditional society (Beck et al, 2003). Part of this process is social reflexivity. This implies that individuals no longer have their lives set out for them or are governed by traditional assumptions and expectations. Both men and women are constantly faced with choices. The establishment of **identity** increasingly becomes a life project of reflexive subjects. According to Giddens (1991), the self is now a constantly reflexive project. As de Jong Gierveld, de Valk and Blommensteijn (2001) note, in the first half of the 20th century, older cohorts of men and women and their life courses could be described by referring to the 'standard biography' or 'semi-standard biography' – these biographies consisted of leaving the parental home to marry, followed by the birth of the first child. Included in these 'standard' biographies is the unwritten social rule that women have the primary responsibility for taking care of children, the elderly, husbands and the household. Parents were assumed to stay together until death. Widowers were to aim at remarriage, while widows were to end their lives living with their children or in a one-person household.

This situation has changed remarkably. Instead of 'standard' biographies, more and more adults are in a position to realise a so-called choice biography (Beck and Beck-Gernsheim, 1996; see also Leccardi and Ruspini, 2006; Thomson, 2008). Transitions no longer follow a standardised, strict sequence. A large variety of pathways through the life course are both possible and accessible. Starting the adult life course with unmarried cohabitation, followed by marriage, followed by divorce, living alone or as a lone parent, followed by unmarried cohabitation with another partner is broadly accepted. The project of the self in the 21st century also increasingly revolves around sexuality, sexual identity and sexual rights (eg Gagnon and Simon, 1973; Kimmel, 2007).

The 20th century saw a radical change in gender roles in the West (Thébaud et al, 1996; Falk, 2009) and female identities have undergone the most intense transformations (see, eg, Jelin, 1990; Hall, 2000; Fraisse et al, 2000; Ruspini and Dale, 2002; Leccardi and Ruspini, 2006; Bock, 2009). At the start of the century, women were denied a voice and a vote and were told that a woman's place was in the home. By the end of it, their position had changed beyond recognition. The Second World War found many women entering the workforce out of necessity; women reassumed the carer position after the war, but, together with cultural shifts leading to the political movements of the 1960s and 1970s, and to the birth control movement, their new-found sense of independence changed the traditional family structure. These processes of emancipation empowered women, leaving them more capable of shaping their own future. We may, for example, speak of women's increasing investment in education; their growing aspirations for self-achievement in work (the condition of financial autonomy is today inalienable); a greater involvement in working life; the possibility to decide regarding reproduction choices; and the free expression of their sexuality. We may also speak of women's growing demand for reciprocity and equality (also at the sexual level) with men, or the increasingly substantial female competition in traditionally 'male' sectors. Women have also become increasingly less willing to deal exclusively with family matters and to devote themselves to partners and children. This decline in motivation is due to women's new competences – with growing schooling rates – and to their increasing presence in the labour market.

Men, along with women, had to rethink and adjust to the changing social environment and expectations. For example, the number of men willing to question the stereotyped model of masculinity is growing (Connell, 1995; Kimmel, 1996).[13] Younger men are beginning to claim a greater share in bringing up their children (see, eg, Dermott, 2008; Featherstone, 2009). A new phenomenon is also emerging on the cultural and symbolic level: the movement for fathers' rights as part of the more general men's rights movement. This refers to those groups aimed at re-conquering the paternal role in the right to custody of children after marital separation and – in some cases – proposing a reformed image of fatherhood (Pease and Pringle, 2001; Ruspini, 2009; Ruspini et al, 2011).

These cultural challenges should be better theorised within family and social policy research (see, eg, Goldsheider and Waite, 1993; Oppenheim Mason and Jensen, 1995; Coltrane, 1998; Hantrais, 2004; Bengtson et al, 2005; Sullivan, 2006; Charles et al, 2008; Gabb, 2008; Lamanna and Riedmann, 2009). Such changes should be of interest for a wide range of policy areas that impact on families, women, men and children.

The book

This book is designed to inform and broaden the debate among students, researchers, family scholars, practitioners and policymakers as to what, today, constitutes family diversity and family change. The book will help the readers discover and understand the characteristics, advantages and drawbacks of contemporary living arrangements and models of parenthood. It will also discuss the political implications – in terms of social movements' characteristics and demands – of these emerging dimensions of social life. The final aim is to contribute to the understanding of individual and family change, opening up new paths for reflection on tensions and challenges linked to the changes in gender identities and family life. This will hopefully be helpful in preparing the new generations of men and women for their encounter with 'other' women and men, and 'other' models of motherhood, fatherhood and families.

The book is divided into six chapters that form two sections: Section One 'Gender change and challenges to intimacy and sexual relations'; and Section Two 'Gender change and challenges to traditional forms of parenthood'. Taking an international perspective, summaries of recent research and a number of data sources from both within and outside government (local and national as well as international sources), the chapters analyse some of the newest forms of femininities and masculinities and their interaction with partnership behaviour, family arrangements and social movements.

The first section of the book (Chapters One to Three) examines the relationship between gender change, forms of intimacy and sexuality. *Chapter One* discusses the issues raised by asexuality (as a form of **sexual orientation**, ie, the 'direction' of one's sexuality and sexual interest) in the process of forming intimate and family relationships. It will also discuss the issues raised by the asexual rights movement, and answer the following questions: 'What is asexuality?'; 'Can asexual people experience parenthood?';' Is there any information that sexual people can learn from asexuals?'; and 'What is the asexual rights movement?'

Chapter Two offers an overview of childfree adults, including: an exploration of what it means to be a childfree man or woman; a discussion of the increasing numbers of childfree adults and what we know about them; and their feelings, motivations and reasons for staying childfree. Finally, it explores the experiences of women who decide not to have children in a culture in which motherhood is central to feminine identity.

Chapter Three discusses the phenomenon of 'living apart together' (LAT). An LAT relationship is a couple, of the same or different gender, that do not live together in the same residence. Partners living in LAT relationships reside in separate households. This is a growing group, which not only is a manifestation of the individualisation and informalisation of relationships, but also reflects the increasing number of couples who attempt to balance **independence**, intimacy and family obligations.

The second section of the book focuses on debates about the impact of gender role changes on parenthood. One of the main questions we will try to answer is the following:'What characteristics make a parent a "good" parent?' Some are widely accepted and involve behaviours such as patience, care, closeness and understanding. About other characteristics, such as the necessity of marriage and heterosexuality, however, a bitter debate has been joined. Here we ask:'Is the capacity for parenthood the direct function of a determinate marital status, a sexual body and a precise sexual orientation?'

Chapter Four explores the phenomenon of househusbands and stay-at-home fathers, men who are becoming more and more numerous, especially in developed Western nations. The househusband role offers economic benefits to the family, and facilitates stable emotional development for children. However, in some countries and regions of the world, the decision to become a stay-at-home husband or father remains culturally unacceptable.

Chapter Five is about lone mothers and lone fathers. The number of lone parents is steadily increasing: the past 15 years has seen a marked increase in the number of lone fathers in many countries such as the US and Great Britain. The chapter will reflect upon forms and characteristics of contemporary lone parenting in Western nations. Social workers are increasingly faced with meeting the needs of lone mothers and fathers and their children.

Chapter Six focuses on lesbian, gay, bisexual and transgender (LGBT) parenting of one or more children. The issues of homosexual and transgender parenting (also trans parenting) will be analysed in detail. 'Homosexual parenting' is a term that includes all those families in which at least one adult, who defines him/herself as homosexual, is the parent (biological or social) of at least one child. Homosexual parenting is an emerging reality in many Western societies, above all following the growing visibility of lesbian mothers living with their partners and their children. Part of the chapter will discuss the situation of gay fathers: although studies of gay fathers and their children have been conducted, less is known about children of gay fathers than about children of lesbian mothers. Equally topical and important is the relationship between parenthood, **transgenderism** (please see the term **transgender** in the glossary) and **transsexuality**. We may speak of transgender parenting when at least one adult, the mother or father of at least one child, decides to make the transition from one gender to the other.

At the end of each chapter we will briefly focus on the relationship between family change and the internet environment. What role do social media and Web 2.0 – the interactive part of the World Wide Web – play in giving visibility to family diversity? Does the Internet platform enable invisible and/or marginalised family forms to be present? The notion of empowering under-represented and misrepresented groups by giving them a voice in the media has been discussed by scholars from a variety of theoretical approaches (see, eg, Couldry, 2008). The unique characteristics of the Internet – its expansiveness, accessibility, inclusivity and decentralised nature – may serve to facilitate the breaking down of traditional power structures (Mazzarella, 2010).

Following Thompson (2005), today, we may speak of a new form of visibility that has become a pervasive feature of the contemporary world and that is linked to the development of communication media. With the development of ICTs, the visibility of individuals, relationships, actions and events is severed from the sharing of a common locale: one no longer has to be present in the same spatial-temporal setting in order to see the other or to witness an action or event. The interpersonal interaction between individuals in Web 2.0 has been specifically valued for its capacity to empower users culturally, socially and politically. Central to Web 2.0 is the requirement for interactive systems to enable the participation of users in production and social interaction (Jarrett, 2008; Anderson, 2012). Involvement in social networking sites has been identified by authors such as Boyd and Jenkins (2006) as necessary for cultural capital. The 'bottom-up' self-organising of the social networking within information sharing sites such as Flickr have been described as challenging the power of elite hierarchies to determine and organise knowledge and practice (Boyd, 2006; Kolbitsch and Maurer, 2006; Schiltz et al, 2007). These practices have been described as 'a revolution', making the Web more democratic and as having the power to disrupt existing cultural, social, political and economic relations (Pascu et al, 2007; for an overview, see Jarrett, 2008). At the end of the book, the readers will find a glossary that provides brief definitions of the key concepts used.

Concerning methodology, we employed a **secondary analysis** approach as a window into a broad range of issues and phenomena affecting individuals and families (Heaton, 1998; Smith, 2006; Boslaugh, 2007; Dale et al, 2008). This approach is based on re-analysis of different data sources: census data; **longitudinal** surveys such as the British Household Panel Survey (BHPS) or the German Socio-economic Panel (GSOEP); the United Nations-coordinated series of Family and Fertility Surveys (FFS) carried out in the mid-1990s across Western and Eastern Europe, and so on. A number of web documents (e-books, online academic Journals, online statistical reports) have been consulted while writing the present book.

In the conclusion, we summarise the characteristics of, and issues raised by, all these new forms of family arrangements, helping push forward our empirical and theoretical understanding of social and individual change within family life. The concluding chapter also looks at the challenges created as a result of these new family forms. Finally, it will look at some of the implications of the findings for social research and for teaching.

Briefly, the aim of the book is to show that, today, it is possible to live, love and form a family without sex, without children, without a shared home, without a partner, without a working husband, without a heterosexual orientation and without a 'natural' (ie biological) sexual body. These are 'new' forms of family life that could help us to move forward by bringing the rigidities, standardisations, constraints and fundamental unsustainability of **modernity** – in terms, for example, of individual and social costs generated by forms of resistance to social change, such as gender discrimination and violence, homophobia, and transphobia – to an end.

Notes

[1] See the Glossary at the end of the book for a presentation of the key concepts used in this introductory chapter (highlighted in bold on first mention).

[2] The exact beginning and ending dates of the Millennial generation are much debated.

[3] In the 2008 US election, Millennials voted for Barack Obama over John McCain by 66% to 32%, while adults ages 30 and over split their votes 50% to 49%. In the four decades since the development of election day exit polling, this is the largest gap ever seen in a presidential election between the votes of those under and over age 30. In 2012, President Obama won re-election primarily because of the support coming from two key, and expanding, constituencies: Hispanics and members of the Millennial generation (see: http://www.pewresearch.org/2009/12/10/the-millennials/ and http://www.forbes.com/sites/joelkotkin/2012/11/07/why-obama-won-hispanics-millenials-were-the-difference-makers/). (Note: all websites cited in this chapter were consulted in the period September–December 2012.)

[4] Beyond the static pages of earlier websites, Web 2.0 is the move towards a more social, collaborative, interactive and responsive Web (Anderson, 2012).

[5] See: http://www.inacol.org/research/docs/national_report.pdf

[6] See: http://www.nasrecruitment.com/docs/white_papers/Generation-Y.p

[7] The term 'contemporary modernity' is used here to create a synthesis of the notions of 'second', 'late', 'high', 'new', or 'post-'modernity.

[8] Not surprisingly, the social sciences (and sociology in particular) emerged as a response to an era of very rapid, all-embracing social changes – namely, the development of capitalism, which destroyed the older forms of social organisation, that is, of the feudal system – and to the consequent need for greater understanding of social, economic and political processes. One begins to study society only when it can no longer be taken for granted (Jedlowski, 1998).

[9] See: http://en.wikipedia.org/wiki/Marriage

[10] See: http://en.wikipedia.org/wiki/LGBT_rights_in_Vatican_City

[11] See: http://en.wikipedia.org/wiki/Late_modernity

[12] A meta-narrative (or 'grand narrative') is a 'story about a story', a comprehensive explanation of historical experience or knowledge that encompasses – and claims to predict – everything. The concept was criticised by Jean-François Lyotard in his work *La condition postmoderne: rapport sur le savoir* [*The postmodern condition: a report on knowledge*] (Lyotard, 1979). The Enlightenment, Marxism and the Catholic doctrine are examples of meta-narratives. Lyotard considered the meta-narrative an essential feature of modernity.

[13.] Michael Kimmel (1995, 1996) calls hegemonic masculinity 'the manhood of racism, of sexism, of homophobia'. Following Kimmel and Aronson (2010), the hegemonic definition of masculinity is constructed in relation to various subordinated masculinities as well as in relation to women. Hegemonic masculinity exists in contrast with that which is feminine. Not only is masculinity rooted in contrast to femininity, it is a complete renunciation of everything feminine.

References

Anderson, K. (2011) 'The Millennial generation', Probe Ministries. Available at: http://www.probe.org/site/c.fdKEIMNsEoG/b.6601055/k.7A91/The_Millennial_Generation.htm

Anderson, P. (2012) *Web 2.0 and beyond: principles and technologies*, London: Chapman & Hall/CRC Textbooks in Computing.

Baca Zinn, M., Eitzen, S.D. and Wells, B. (2010) *Diversity in families*, London: Pearson Education.

Badinter, E. (1981) *Mother love: myth and reality: motherhood in modern history*, Basingstoke: Palgrave MacMillan.

Balduzzi, P. and Rosina, A. (2009) 'Competent, qualified, technological: in search of a new form of citizenship. Brain drain in Italy', paper presented at the Conference Nomad Power. Values, Illusions, Aspirations of Errant Youth, Rimini.

Barnard, K.E. and Martell, L.K. (1995) 'Mothering', in M. Bornstein (ed) *Handbook of parenting, vol. 3: status and social conditioning of parenting*, Hove: Erlbaum, pp 3–26.

Bauman, Z. (1992) *Intimations of postmodernity*, London and New York, NY: Routledge.

Beck, U. (1992) *Risk society: towards a new modernity*, London: Sage Publications.

Beck, U. and Beck-Gernsheim, E. (1995) *The normal chaos of love*, Cambridge: Polity Press.

Beck, U. and Beck-Gernsheim, E. (1996) 'Individualization and precarious freedoms: perspectives and controversies of a subject-orientated sociology', in P. Heelas, S. Lash and P. Morris (eds) *Detraditionalization: critical reflections of authority and identity*, Oxford: Blackwell, pp 22–48.

Beck, U. and Beck-Gernsheim, E. (2001) *Individualization. Institutionalized individualism and its social and political consequences*, London: Sage Publications.

Beck, U. and Grande, E. (2010) 'Varieties of second modernity: the cosmopolitan turn in social and political theory and research', *British Journal of Sociology*, vol 61, no 3, pp 409–43.

Beck, U., Bonß, W. and Lau, C. (2003) 'The theory of reflexive modernization: problematic, hypotheses and research programme', *Theory, Culture & Society*, vol 20, no 2, pp 1–33.

Becker, G. (1981) *A treatise on the family*, Cambridge, MA: Harvard University Press.

Beck-Gernsheim, E. (2002) *Reinventing the family. In search of new lifestyles*, Cambridge: Polity Press.

Benadusi, L. (2012) *The enemy of the new man, homosexuality in fascist Italy*, Madison, WI: University of Wisconsin Press.

Bengtson, V.L., Acock, A.C., Allen, K.R., Dilworth-Anderson, P. and Klein, D.M. (eds) (2005) *Sourcebook of family theory and research*, Thousands Oaks, CA: Sage Publications.

Berger, P.L. (1999) 'The desecularization of the world: a global overview', in P.L. Berger (ed) *The desecularization of the world, resurgent religion in world politics*, Washington: Ethics and Public Policy Center, pp 1–18.

Berger, P.L. and Kellner, H. (1964) 'Marriage and the construction of reality: an exercise in the microsociology of knowledge', *Diogenes*, vol 12, no 46, pp 1–25.

Bernstein, F.L. (2007) *The dictatorship of sex: lifestyle advice for the soviet masses*, DeKalb, IL: Northern Illinois University Press.

Bock, G. (2009) *Women in European history (making of Europe)*, Oxford: Wiley-Blackwell.

Boslaugh, S. (2007) *Secondary data sources for public health: a practical guide*, New York, NY: Cambridge University Press.

Boyd, D. (2006) 'Identity production in a networked culture: why youth heart MySpace', American Association for the Advancement of Science, St. Louis, 19 February. Available at: http://www.danah.org/papers/AAAS2006.html

Boyd, D. and Jenkins, H. (2006) 'MySpace and Deleting Online Predators Act (DOPA)', *MIT Tech Talk*, 26 May. Available at: http://www.danah.org/papers/MySpaceDOPA.html

Browning, G., Halcli, A. and Webster, F. (eds) (2000) *Understanding contemporary society: theories of the present*, London: Sage Publications.

CDF (Congregatio pro Doctrina Fidei – Congregation for the Doctrine of the Faith) (2003) 'Considerations regarding proposals to give legal recognition to unions between homosexual persons, Rome'. Available at: http://www.vatican.va/roman_curia/congregations/cfaith/documents/rc_con_cfaith_doc_20030731_homosexual-unions_en.html

Charles, N., Davies, C. and Harris, C. (2008) *Families in transition: social change, family formation and kin relationships*, Bristol: The Policy Press.

Cherlin, A.J. (2007) 'The deinstitutionalization of american marriage', in S. Ferguson (ed) *Shifting the center: understanding contemporary families* (3rd edn), New York, NY: McGraw Hill, pp 183–201.

CIC (Congregatio pro Istitutione Catholica – Congregation for Catholic Education) (1983) 'Educational guidance in human love. Outlines for sex education'. Available at: http://www.vatican.va/roman_curia/congregations/ccatheduc/documents/rc_con_ccatheduc_doc_19831101_sexual-education_en.html

Cipolla, C. (ed) (1996) *Sul letto di Procuste. Introduzione alla sociologia della sessualità (The bed of Procustes. Introduction to the study of sexuality)*, Milano: FrancoAngeli.

Coltrane, S. (1998) *Gender and families*, Thousand Oaks, CA: Pine Forge Press.

Connell, R.W. (1995) *Masculinities*, Berkeley, CA: University of California Press.

Couldry, N. (2008) 'Media and the problem of voice', in N. Carpentier and B. de Cleen (eds) *Participation and media production*, Cambridge: Scolars Press, pp 15–24.

Crompton, R. (1997) *Women and work in modern Britain*, New York, NY: Oxford University Press.

Dale, A., Wathan J. and Higgins, V. (2008) 'Secondary analysis of quantitative data sources', in P. Alasuutari, L. Bickman and J. Brannen (eds) *The SAGE handbook of social research methods*, Newbury Park, CA: Sage, pp 520–35.

De Grazia, V. (1992) *How fascism ruled women 1922–1943*, Berkeley, CA: University of California Press.

De Jong Gierveld, J., de Valk H. and Blommesteijn, M. (2001) 'Living arrangements of older persons and family support in more developed countries'. Available at: http://www.un.org/esa/population/publications/bulletin42_43/dejong_gierveld.pdf

Demo, DH., Allen, K.R. and Fine, M.A. (2000) *Handbook of family diversity*, New York, NY: Oxford University Press.

Dermott, E. (2008) *Intimate fatherhood: a sociological analysis*, London and New York, NY: Routledge.

Di Nicola, P. (1983) 'Infanzia e politica sociale: due immagini a confronto' ('Childhood and social policies'), in P. Donati (ed) *Infanzia e salute. Prospettive sociologiche e sanitarie*, Milano: FrancoAngeli.

Eisenstadt, S.N. (ed) (2005) *Multiple modernities*, New Brunswick/London: Transaction Publishers.

Erera, P.I. (2002) *Family diversity: continuity and change in the contemporary family*, London: Sage Publications.

Falk, G. (2009) *Women and social change in America: a survey of a century of progress*, Jefferson, NC: McFarland and Company, Incorporated Publishers.

Featherstone, B. (2009) *Contemporary fathering: theory, policy and practice*, Bristol: The Policy Press.

Forcucci, L.E. (2010) 'Battle for births: the fascist pronatalist campaign in Italy 1925 to 1938', *Journal of the Society for the Anthropology of Europe*, vol 10, no 1, pp 4–13. Available at: http://onlinelibrary.wiley.com/doi/10.1111/j.1556-5823.2010.00002.x/pdf

Fraisse, G., Duby, G. and Perrot, M. (2000) *History of women in the West, volume IV: emerging feminism from revolution to world war*, Cambridge, MA: Harvard University Press.

Gabb, J. (2008) *Researching intimacy in families*, Basingstoke: Palgrave MacMillan.

Gagnon, J.H. and Simon, W. (1973) *Sexual conduct: the social sources of human sexuality*, London: Hutchinson & Co. Ltd.

Giddens, A. (1990) *The consequences of modernity*, Cambridge: Polity Press.

Giddens, A. (1991) *Modernity and self-identity. Self and society in the late modern age*, Cambridge: Polity Press.

Giddens, A. (1992) *The transformation of intimacy: sexuality, love, and eroticism in modern societies*, Cambridge: Polity Press.

Giles, J. (2004) *The parlour and the suburb: domestic identities, class, femininity and modernity*, Oxford: Berg.

Goldscheider, F.K. and Waite, L.J. (1993) *New families, no families? The transformation of the American home*, Berkeley, CA: University of California Press.

Gori, G. (1999) 'Model of masculinity: Mussolini, the "new Italian" of the fascist era', *International Journal of the History of Sport*, vol 16, no 4, pp 27–61.

Greenberg, E.H. and Weber, K. (2008) *Generation we: how Millennial youth are taking over America and changing our world forever*, Pachatusan: LLC.

Hackstaff, K.B. (1999) *Marriage in a culture of divorce*, Philadelphia, PA: Temple University Press.

Haferkamp, H. and Smelser, N.J. (eds) (1992) *Social change and modernity*, Berkeley and Los Angeles, CA: University of California Press. Available at: http://publishing.cdlib.org/ucpressebooks/view?docId=ft6000078s&chunk.id=d0e313&toc.depth=1&toc.id=d0e313&brand=ucpress;query=autonomy#1

Hall, L.A. (2000) *Sex, gender and social change in Britain since 1880*, European Culture and Society Series, Basingstoke: Palgrave Macmillan.

Hantrais, L. (2004) *Family policy matters: responding to family change in Europe*, Bristol: The Policy Press.

Harvey, D. (1989) *The condition of postmodernity: an enquiry into the origins of cultural change*, Oxford: Basil Blackwell.

Heaton, J. (1998) 'Secondary analysis of qualitative data', *Social Research Update*, 22. Available at: http://sru.soc.surrey.ac.uk/SRU22.html

Hoffman, J. (2004) *Citizenship beyond the state*, London: Sage.

Howe, N. and Strauss W. (2000) *Millennials rising: the next great generation*, New York, NY: Vintage Books.

Irving, Z. (2008) 'Gender and work', in D. Richardson and V. Robinson (eds) *Introducing gender and women's studies*, Basingstoke: Palgrave MacMillan.

Jameson, F. (1991) *Postmodernism, or, the cultural logic of late capitalism*, Durham, NC: Duke University Press.

Janssens, A. (2002) *Family and social change: the household as a process in an industrializing community*, New York, NY: Cambridge University Press.

Jarrett, K. (2008) 'Interactivity is evil! A critical investigation of Web 2.0', *First Monday*, vol 13, no 3, 3 March. Available at: http://firstmonday.org/htbin/cgiwrap/bin/ojs/index.php/fm/article/view/2140/1947

Jedlowski, P. (1998) *Il mondo in questione. Introduzione alla storia del pensiero sociologico (A world that cannot be taken for granted. An introduction to the history of sociology)*, Roma: Carocci.

Jelin, E. (1990) *Women and social change in Latin America*, New York, NY: Zed Books.

Kapella, O., Rille-Pfeiffer, C., Rupp, M. and Schneider, N.F. (eds) (2010) *Family diversity: collection of the 3rd European Congress of Family Science*, Berlin: Barbara Budrich Publishers.

Keeter, S. and Taylor, P. (2009) *The Millennials, numbers, facts and trends shaping your world*, Washington DC: Pew Research Center. Available at: http://www.pewresearch.org/2009/12/10/the-millennials/

Kimmel, M.S. (1995) *The politics of manhood*, Philadelphia, PA: Temple University Press.

Kimmel, M.S. (1996) *Manhood in America. A cultural history*, New York, NY: Free Press.

Kimmel, M.S. (ed) (2007) *The sexual self: the construction of sexual scripts*, Nashville, TN: Vanderbilt University Press.

Kimmel, M.S. and Aronson, A. (2010) *The gendered society reader* (4th edn), New York, NY: Oxford University Press.

Klett-Davies, M. (2007) *Going it alone? Lone motherhood in late modernity*, Aldershot: Ashgate.

Kolbitsch, J. and Maurer, H. (2006) 'The transformation of the Web: how emerging communities shape the information we consume', *Journal of Universal Computer Science*, vol 12, no 2, pp 187–213.

Lamanna, M.A. and Riedmann, A. (2009) *Marriages & families: making choices in a diverse society*, Belmont: Thomson Wadsworth.

Leccardi, C. and Ruspini, E. (eds) (2006) *A new youth? Young people, generations and family life*, Aldershot: Ashgate Publishing.

Lindsey, L.L. (2010) *Gender roles: a sociological perspective* (3rd edn), Upper Saddle River, NJ: Pearson Higher Education.

Lorber, J. (2000) 'Using gender to undo gender: a feminist degendering movement', *Feminist Theory*, vol 1, no 1, pp 79–95.

Luckmann, T. (1967) *The invisible religion: the problem of religion in modern society*, New York, NY: Macmillan.

Lyotard, J.-F. (1979) *La condition postmoderne: rapport sur le savoir*, Paris: Minuit (English translation: Lyotard, J.-F. [1984] *The postmodern condition: a report on knowledge*, Manchester: Manchester University Press).

Macfarlane, A. (1987) 'Love and capitalism', in A. Macfarlane (ed) *The culture of capitalism*, Oxford: Blackwell. Available at: http://www.alanmacfarlane.com/TEXTS/LOVE_long.pdf

Mazzarella, S.R. (ed) (2010) *Girl Wide Web. Revisiting girls, the Internet, and the negotiation of identity*, Series Mediated Youth, vol 9, New York, NY: Peter Lang.

Mintz, S. and Kellogg, S. (1998) *Domestic revolutions. A social history of American family life*, New York, NY: The Free Press.

Mosse, G.L. (1998) *The image of man: the creation of modern masculinity*, New York, NY: Oxford University Press.

Murray, J. (ed) (2001) *Love, marriage and family in the middle ages: a reader*, Toronto: University of Toronto Press.

Oinonen, E. (2008) *Families in converging Europe. A comparison of forms, structures and ideas*, Basingstoke: Palgrave Macmillan.

Oppenheim Mason, J. and Jensen, A.-M. (eds) (1995) *Gender and family change in industrialized countries*, New York, NY: Clarendon Press.

Parke, R.D. (1995) 'Fathers and families', in M. Bornstein (ed) *Handbook of parenting, vol. 3, status and social conditioning of parenting*, Hove: Erlbaum, pp 27–63.

Parsons, T. (1943) 'The kinship system of the contemporary United States', *American Anthropologist* (New Series), vol 45, no 1, pp 22–38.

Parsons, T. (1954) *Essays in sociological theory*, New York, NY: Free Press.

Pascu, C., Osimo, D., Ulbrich, M., Turlea, G. and Burgelman, J.C. (2007) 'The potential disruptive impact of Internet 2 based technologies', *First Monday*, vol 12, no 3 (March). Available at: http://journals.uic. edu/fm/article/view/1630/1545

Pease, B. and Pringle, K. (eds) (2001) *A man's world? Changing men's practices in a globalized world*, London: Zed Books.

Rainer, T. and Rainer, J. (2011) *The Millennials: connecting to America's largest generation*, Nashville, TN: B&H Publishing Group.

Robinson, V. and Hockey, J. (2011) *Masculinities in transition*, Basingstoke: Palgrave MacMillan.

Rousseau, C.M. and Rosenthal, J.T. (eds) (1998) *Women, marriage, and family in medieval Christendom: essays in memory of Michael M. Sheehan, C.S.B.*, Kalamazoo, MI: Medieval Institute Publications, Western Michigan University.

Ruspini, E. (2009) 'Italian forms of masculinity between familism and social change', *Culture, Society and Masculinities*, vol 1, no 2, pp 121–36.

Ruspini, E. and Dale, A. (eds) (2002) *The gender dimension of social change. The contribution of dynamic research to the study of women's life courses*, Bristol: The Policy Press.

Ruspini, E., Hearn, J., Pease, B. and Pringle, K. (eds) (2011) *Men and masculinities around the world. Transforming men's practices*, Global Masculinities Series, Basingstoke: Palgrave Macmillan.

Schiltz, M., Truyen, F. and Coppens, H. (2007) 'Cutting the trees of knowledge: social software, information architecture and their epistemic consequences', *Thesis Eleven*, no 89, May, pp 94–114.

Scott, C.V. (1995) *Gender and development: rethinking modernization and dependency theory*, Boulder, CO: Lynne Rienner Publishers.

Smith, E. (2006) *Using secondary data in educational and social research*, Milton Keynes: Open University Press.

Stanton, G.T. and Hess, A. (2012) 'Generational values and desires', Focus on the Family Findings. Available at: http://www.focusonthefamily.com/about_us/focus-findings/family-formation-trends/generational-values-desires.aspx

Sullivan, O. (2006) *Changing gender relations, changing families: tracing the pace of change over time*, Lanham, MD: Rowman and Littlefield.

Taylor, P. and Keeter, S. (eds) (2010) *Millennials: a portrait of generation next. Confident, connected, open to change*, February, Washington DC: Pew Research Center. Available at: http://www.pewsocialtrends.org/files/2010/10/millennials-confident-connected-open-to-change.pdf

Taylor-Gooby, P. (2005) 'Pervasive uncertainty in second modernity: an empirical test', *Sociological Research Online*, vol 10, no 4. Available at: http://www.socresonline.org.uk/10/4/taylor-gooby.html

Thébaud, F., Duby, G. and Perrot, P. (1996) *A history of women in the West: toward a cultural identity in the twentieth century*, Cambridge, MA: Harvard University Press.

Thompson, J.B. (2005) 'The new visibility', *Theory, Culture and Society*, vol 22, no 6, pp 31–51. Available at: http://tcs.sagepub.com/cgi/content/abstract/22/6/31

Thompson, R. (2008), *Unfolding lives. Youth, gender and change*, Bristol: The Policy Press.

Tilly, L.A. and Scott, J.W (1987) *Women, work, and family*, London and New York, NY: Routledge.

Touraine, A. (2005) *Un nouveau paradigme, pour comprendre le monde aujourd'hui*, Paris: Fayard (English translation: Touraine, A. [2007] *New paradigm for understanding today's world*, New York, NY: John Wiley and Sons).

Venkatesh, A., Dholakia, R.R. and Dholakia, N. (1995) 'New visions of information technology and postmodernism: implications for advertising and marketing communications', in W. Brenner and L. Kolbe (eds) *The information superhighway and private households: case studies of business impacts*, Heidelberg: Physical-Verlag, pp 319–25.

Watt, I.P. (1957) *The rise of the novel: studies in Defoe, Richardson and Fielding*, Berkeley and Los Angeles, CA: University of California Press.

Weber, M. (1946) *Essays in sociology*, New York, NY: Oxford University Press.

Westermarck, E. (1921) *The history of human marriage*, London: MacMillan.

Williams, F. (2004) *Rethinking families*, London: Calouste Gulbenkian Foundation.

Wilson, B.R. (1982) *Religion in sociological perspective*, New York, NY: Oxford University Press.

Wood, E. M. (1996) 'Modernity, postmodernity, or capitalism?', *Monthly Review*, vol 48, no 3, pp 21-39. Available at: http://www.highbeam.com/doc/1G1-18484828.html

Zemon Davis, N., Farge, A., Duby, G. and Perrot, M. (1993) *History of women in the West, volume III: Renaissance and the Enlightenment paradoxes*, Cambridge, MA: Harvard University Press.

Section One

Gender change and challenges to
intimacy and sexual relations

CHAPTER ONE

Asexual women and men: living without sex

Asexuality: a complex concept

Our first chapter is devoted to asexuality. This may appear a weird choice, as the relationship between asexuality and children is not obvious. However, in our opinion, children and marriage are not choices determined by **sexual orientation**. As we will shortly see, asexual people are as capable of experiencing love and becoming parents as anyone else.

What is asexuality? Is it a dysfunction, an orientation or a choice? How many people define themselves as 'asexual'? Can asexual people have a relationship and a family? Can asexual people be ('good') parents? What has asexuality to do with families?

It is not easy to define *asexuality*. Numerous definitions have been suggested, but no single definition of asexuality is accepted by everyone or even by a majority of people, social scientists and researchers. First of all, asexuality has been portrayed in a negative light, as a minus involving 'a lack of sexual attraction', 'deficient sexual desire' or 'deviation' from the 'normal'. Researchers have often used the term to refer to individuals with *low* or *absent* sexual desire or attractions, *low* or *absent* sexual behaviours, *exclusively romantic* non-sexual partnerships, or a combination of both *absent* sexual desires and behaviours. Asexuality has also been defined as an enduring *lack* of sexual attraction or the *denial* of one's 'natural' sexuality, a *disorder* caused by *shame* of sexuality or anxiety. According to Storms (1980), asexuality is a *lack of sexual orientation*. As Haefner (2011) notes, asexuality has been defined in many ways, including: a stage of sexual behaviour characterised by 'unexpressed sexuality' (Johnson and Johnson, 1963, p 52); a preferred state of 'non-sexual activity' (Johnson, 1977; Nurius, 1983; Rothblum and Brehony, 1993); a state of 'low sexual fantasy' (Storms, 1980); a 'sexual orientation based on lack', the 'lack of arousal from erotic materials', the 'lack of love of either sex', the 'lack of sexual attraction to either sex' and the 'lack of sexual activity with either sex' (Berkey et al, 1990); a sexual orientation based on sexual attraction to *neither* sex (Sell, 1996); and *lack* of sexual interest due to diet and *repression* of desire (Carlat et al, 1997). Others argue that asexuality reflects a *denial* of one's natural sexuality, and/or that it is a *disorder* caused by *shame of sexuality* or *anxiety*.

An asexual woman or man has thus been defined as a person who has engaged in *few* or *no* sexual behaviours (Rothblum and Brehony, 1993), has *low* sexual desire, has both *little* sexual experience and *low* sexual desire, and has *no* 'attraction' to men or to women (Nurius, 1983). Yet, some scholars have recently used the term in a broader and richer way (see, eg, Prause and Graham, 2007; Kim, 2010). Although empirical research on asexuality reveals lower self-reported sexual desire and arousal and lower rates of sexual activity, the speculation that there may also be an impaired psycho-physiological sexual arousal response has never been tested. On the contrary, a study by Brotto and Yule (2011)[1] based on a sample of 38 women between the ages of 19 and 55 years (10 heterosexual, 10 bisexual, 11 homosexual and seven asexual) suggests 'normal' subjective and physiological sexual arousal capacity in asexual women, challenging the view that asexuality should be characterised as a sexual dysfunction.

Increasingly, scholars have begun to consider asexuality as a fourth category of **sexual orientation**,[2] the 'direction' of one's sexual interest, distinct from heterosexuality, homosexuality or bisexuality (see, eg, Melby, 2005; Carrigan, 2011). In fact, gay, lesbian, bisexual or trans individuals may also be asexual. And while asexuality reflects an orientation to sexual practice, it does not preclude romantic attraction. Thus, homo–romantics (individuals attracted to members of the same-sex), hetero–romantics (individuals attracted to members of the opposite sex), omni–romantics (whose attractions are not based on sex or gender) and trans–romantics (who are attracted to **transgender** or intersex individuals), might forgo the option of having sexual relations.

However, an asexual may also be defined as person who is not sexually attracted to anyone of any gender, a person who does not experience sexual attraction (Scherrer, 2008, p 626). Asexual individuals do not find (and perhaps never have found) others sexually appealing; they may have sexual attraction to others, but indicate little or no desire for sexual activity. Finally, asexuality should be differentiated from abstinence and celibacy, which are generally motivated by factors such as personal values or religious orientation.

It is important to remember that sexuality and its attendant practices and rules vary from **culture** to culture, vary over time and vary over the course of each of our lives. So, for example, moral standards governing sex and sexuality have changed considerably over time in

Western culture (see the introductory chapter for details). Sexuality is a socially constructed dimension of the **life course**, and it represents only one form of **intimacy**. It is learned in roughly the same way as many other behaviours are learned. Just as women and men are socialised to learn how to behave appropriately (eg how to behave in different contexts), they are socialised to become sexual in certain ways (Caplan, 1987; Giddens, 1992; Lorber, 1994; Fracher and Kimmel, 2005). Moreover, sexuality is many-sided, and may be studied from the biological, emotional, physical, sociological, cultural, political, legal, philosophical, moral, ethical, theological, spiritual or religious points of view. The Asexual Visibility and Education Network (AVEN; see later for details)[3] defines an asexual as 'someone who does not experience sexual attraction'. And while 'there is no litmus test to determine if someone is asexual' a 'small minority will think of themselves as asexual for a brief period of time, while exploring and questioning their own sexuality'. Asexuality is like any other identity, 'at its core, it is just a word that people use to help figure themselves out.... If at any point someone finds the word asexual useful to describe themselves, we encourage them to use it for as long as it makes sense to do so'.[4]

Clearly, then, asexual women and men are not a homogeneous group: indeed, there are significant differences, based on age, generation, class, ethnicity and so on, among them. Yet, they have the same emotional needs as anyone else and, as is the case in the sexually active community, they vary widely in how they achieve fulfilment.[5] As is the case for sexually active individuals, asexuals vary in their experience of relationships, attraction and the circumstances of erotic experience and arousal. For example, some individuals who identify as asexual have reported that they feel sexual attraction but are not inclined to act on those feelings because they have neither the desire nor the need for sexual engagement (nor, in some cases, amorous exchanges such as cuddling, hand-holding, etc).

There are indeed many non-sexual ways to be intimate with a partner, including: the sharing of feelings; discussing, talking and listening; spending time together; and participating in common interests and activities (Miller and Perlman, 2008; Strong et al, 2008). In other words, an asexual person may be defined as a person (male or female) who is not erotically excited by thoughts or the sights of a human body in the way a heterosexual (or homosexual or bisexual) person is. For these reasons, it is possible to argue that the term *a*sexuality may not be appropriate, as it only implies the lack of *one* of the dimensions of sexuality.

Existing research makes clear that asexuals can and do have sexual intercourse; they just do not experience sexual desire (Bogaert, 2004, 2006, 2012; Prause and Graham, 2007; Scherrer, 2008; Brotto et al, 2010; Haefner, 2011). Some asexuals engage in sexual activity for a variety of reasons. For example, they might want to lead what they see as a 'normal' life: find a partner, marry or have children (Prause and Graham, 2004). Asexual people also differ in their feelings towards performing sex acts: some are indifferent, while some tolerate sex in an effort to please a non-asexual partner. Some asexual men and women participate in sexual activity out of curiosity. Others are more strongly averse to the idea even though they do not necessarily dislike other people for having sex as long as it does not involve them. Some may masturbate, while others do not feel a need to do so. The studies by Brotto et al (2010), based both on quantitative and qualitative data,[6] show that sexual response was lower than normative data, but masturbation frequency in males was similar to available data for sexual men. The findings also suggest that asexuals vary greatly in their experience of sexual response and practice. Asexuals partnered with sexuals acknowledged having to 'negotiate' sexual activity. There was no evidence of higher rates of psychopathology among asexuals. There was also strong opposition to viewing asexuality as an 'extreme' case of sexual desire disorder. Finally, asexuals were very motivated to liaise with researchers to further the scientific study of asexuality.

Asexuality is thus lived plurally. As with any sexual orientation, what is considered 'asexual' ranges widely, and there is a huge variety in the experiences of people who identify as asexual. As Scherrer (2008, p 634) suggests in her study on asexual identity and community, asexuality is complexly and variably lived among asexuals, so that some are not interested in any romantic physical contact, while others simply are not interested in coital sex.

Considering asexuality as an identity category requires us to proceed cautiously, and to reject oversimplified definitions. Asexuality also allows us to understand how people can negotiate the social pressures around sex and sexuality in relationships. We live in an oversexed culture: the constant flux of sexual messages and stimuli may create desires that cannot be satisfied. This may lead to a loss of interest in sexual relations. As Przybylo (2011, p 444) writes, 'asexuality also provides an exciting forum for revisiting questions of sexual normativity and examining those sex acts which are cemented to appear "natural" through repetition, in the discursive system of sexusociety'.

Thus, asexuality may be somewhat of a question in itself for scholars of gender and sexuality. Cerankowski and Milks (2010), who address asexuality by means of feminist and **queer** studies, argue that it raises many more questions than it resolves, for example, how and why an individual might both desire and find the ability to abstain from having sex, which is generally accepted by society to be the most 'natural' of instincts.

Due to this complexity, the term 'asexual' has received very little research attention until now. Academic interest in asexual people is new and researchers are beginning to discuss how to proceed methodologically and conceptually with the study of asexuality (Bogaert, 2004; DeLuzio Chasin, 2011). The explicit sociological theorising of sexuality has a relatively short history, dating back to the late 1960s. Before that time, there had been only some attention to the social ordering of sexual relations and a few empirical studies of sexual behaviour. Sexuality itself, however, was rarely questioned; indeed, it was treated largely as a given, something that could be regulated by social institutions and conventions, but was itself a pre-social fact (Jackson and Scott, 2010).

Research on asexuality

How many people are asexual? Following a number of studies, approximately 1% of the population self-identifies as asexual. Alfred Kinsey, the 'father' of sexology, was aware of an 'asexual element' in the population. In both the *Male* and *Female* volumes of the Kinsey Reports (Kinsey et al, 1948, 1953), an additional grade, listed as 'X', was added to the Kinsey scale[7] and used for asexuality. Alfred Kinsey labelled 1.5% of the adult male population as 'X' in the first book; in his second book (*Sexual behaviour in the human female*; Kinsey et al, 1953), he reported the following breakdown of individuals graded as 'X': unmarried females = 14–19%; married females = 1–3%; previously married females = 5–8%; unmarried males = 3–4%; married males = 0%; previously married males = 1–2%.

The first study providing empirical data on asexuals was published in 1983 by Paula Nurius. Nurius focused on the relationship between sexual orientation and mental health. Unlike previous researchers, she used a variant of Kinsey's two-dimensional model of sexual orientation. A total of 689 women and men – most of whom were students at various universities in the US taking psychology or sociology classes – were contacted and asked how frequently they engaged in various sexual activities and how often they would like to engage in those activities. Based on the results, respondents were given a score ranging from 0 to 100 for hetero-eroticism and from 0 to 100 for homoeroticism. The 5% of male and 10% of female respondents who scored lower than 10 on both were labelled 'asexual'. Questionnaire responses indicated that asexual respondents were more likely to have low self-esteem and more likely to be depressed than other students; 25.88% of heterosexuals, 26.54% of bisexuals (called 'ambisexuals'), 29.88% of homosexuals and 33.57% of asexuals were reported to have problems with self-esteem. A similar trend existed for depression. Paula Nurius did not think that firm conclusions could be drawn from her study for a variety of reasons.

To begin with, asexuals reported not only a much lower frequency of, but also a much lower desire for, a variety of actual and fantasised sexual activities, including: multiple partners, anal sex, sexual encounters in unusual settings and engagement in autoerotic activities.

Further empirical data about an asexual demographic appeared in 1994, when a research team in the UK carried out a comprehensive survey of 18,876 British residents, spurred by the need for sexual information in the wake of the AIDS pandemic. The survey included a question on sexual attraction, to which 1.05% of the respondents replied that they had 'never felt sexually attracted to anyone at all' (Wellings, 1994).

In a later study based on data from the 2002 National Survey of Family Growth (NSFG)[8] to ascertain and analyse patterns of asexuality in the US (Poston and Baumle, 2010), almost 5% of the women and more than 6% of the men surveyed reported that they had never had sexual intercours. With respect to sexual attraction, almost 1% each of both women (0.8%) and men (0.7%) were 'not sure' about their sexual orientation. As argued earlier, this would be the likely response of persons who are asexual, although the category would include other individuals as well.

Most recently, Canadian sexuality researcher Anthony Bogaert explored the asexual demographic in a series of studies. In his well-known work, Bogaert (2004) used data from a national probability sample ($n > 18,000$) of British residents to investigate asexuality, defined as having no sexual attraction to a partner of either sex. Approximately 1% ($n = 195$) of the sample indicated that they were asexual. The results suggest that a number of pathways, both biological and psychosocial, contribute to the development of asexuality. On average, asexuals had fewer sexual partners than sexual people, started having sex later (if at all) and were currently having less sex. They were less likely to currently be in a cohabiting or married relationship. Asexuals were also older than people who were sexually active. They were more likely to be female, poor, non-white and/or poorly educated. In addition,

Bogaert reported that, on average, asexuals attended religious services more often than sexuals.

Asexuality, couples, children

In general, being asexual has no relation to whether one has children or not. Thus, asexuals may have children, or they may be childfree by either choice or circumstance. There are no biological impediments that prevent an asexual individual (man or woman) from reproducing. That is, being asexual, in and of itself, has nothing to do with reproduction. And, to date, no one has shown any correlation between asexuality and infertility. Asexual women and men are as capable of having children as anyone else, and many appear to want to become mothers or fathers.

How is it possible to be a parent and, at the same time, an asexual individual? Just like anyone else, asexual individuals can choose to have sex for the purpose of bearing children, use reproductive technologies or seek to adopt a child.

The case of asexual men and women who choose to use reproductive technologies for the purpose of becoming parents is particularly interesting. As Kindregan (2006) notes, the availability of **assisted reproductive technology** (ART) has created the potential for new family forms, which now coexist with traditional marriages. In addition, in recent years, there has been increasing acceptance of parenting opportunities for persons living in non-traditional family settings, including non-marital unions, same-sex unions, single-parent families and other relationships that do not track the traditional nuclear family model.[9] When combined, these two developments have created new forms of parenting, including gamete-donor and donor parents, embryo transfer parents, gestational **surrogate mothers** (please see the term **surrogate motherhood** in the Glossary), intended non-genetic or social parents, and so on (see, eg, Golombok et al, 2002; Scheib et al, 2003, 2005; Markens, 2007; Freeman et al, 2009; Teman, 2011). Today, parenthood is not always dependent upon sexual relationships and sexual intercourse. Here, the concept of 'social parenthood' becomes a crucial one. This role encompasses the love, care and support of parents for children who are not necessarily their biological offspring.

Thus, the ability to have children by assisted reproduction presents new challenges to the legislatures and courts and has created the need for legal categories that did not previously exist. Courts should now consider whether the traditional categories of 'mother' and 'father' can no longer be universally applied (Kindregan, 2006).

The asexual movement

Until recently, asexuality was generally seen as a disorder (comparable to Hypoactive Sexual Desire Disorder; HSDD[10]) based on either a psychological or a biochemical disorder: for instance, a past trauma such as abuse or a hormonal disorder. As we have seen, today, there is a growing recognition that asexuality is not a disorder, but a sexual orientation like heterosexuality or homosexuality, and should be respected as such.

Although there is some prejudice against asexual individuals, it is probably different from the 'phobia' that lesbians and gay men experience. Because most people genuinely do not understand asexuality, it is likely that when asexual individuals report discrimination, it is probably a consequence of marginalisation. Asexuals are not oppressed for being asexual; they are, rather, invisible. Nonetheless, they do also have representation among the oppressed. For example, asexuals who are also transgender experience discrimination as **transgender** individuals. Or, asexuals who would prefer to have partners of the same gender are likely to be read as gay and treated accordingly. Asexual individuals do, however, face similar problems as homosexuals and bisexuals in making decisions about **coming out** (publicly declaring their sexual orientation). Otherwise, though, the main difficulties asexuals face is a lack of understanding, as some people are ignorant about asexuality, refuse to acknowledge it or insist that something is wrong with the asexual person that can and should be fixed (Davies, 1992; Jenness, 1992).

What role do social media and the Web 2.0 play in giving a voice to asexuals? In order to combat this 'invisibility', AVEN[11] was created. AVEN was founded in 2001 by David Jay with two primary goals: to create public acceptance and discussion of asexuality; and to facilitate the growth of an asexual community. Since that time, it has grown to host the world's largest online asexual community, serving as an informational resource and meeting place for people who are asexual, their friends and families, academic researchers, and the press. The network has additional satellite communities in 10 languages. Members of AVEN have been involved in media coverage spanning television, print and radio and participate in lectures, conferences and 'Pride' events around the world.

Asexual communities such as AVEN can be beneficial to those aiming to resolve a crisis of identity. The increasing availability of resources like AVEN facilitates identification with a larger community. After individuals realise that their sexual inclinations differ from those of most of their peers, they may experience a period of severe emotional distress, questioning why they feel this way and whether the way they feel is acceptable. In some cases, they may seek medical help because they feel that they have a disease. In this context, the existence of asexuality support groups provides support and information that allows newly identified asexuals to find a community that defines their orientation as acceptable. Currently, asexual organisations and other Internet resources play a key role in informing people about asexuality. For example, the AVEN website offers answers to the most frequently asked questions about asexuality.[12] If a question is not on the list, people can post it on the free web hosting forum.

We should also mention the Asexual Awareness Week (AAW),[13] an international organisation dedicated to raising awareness and visibility about the asexual spectrum worldwide. The AAW launched the Asexual Community Census 2011[14] as part of the preparation for Asexual Awareness Week 2011 (23–29 October), a census of the asexual community was held: 3,436 self-identified asexual people responded.

Notes

[1] The aim of the study was to compare genital (vaginal pulse amplitude; VPA) and subjective sexual arousal in asexual and non-asexual women. Thirty-eight women between the ages of 19 and 55 years (10 heterosexual, 10 bisexual, 11 homosexual and seven asexual) viewed neutral and erotic audio-visual stimuli while VPA and self-reported sexual arousal and affect were measured. There were no significant group differences in the increased VPA and self-reported sexual arousal response to the erotic film between the groups. Asexuals showed significantly less positive affect, sensuality-sexual attraction and self-reported autonomic arousal to the erotic film compared to the other groups; however, there were no group differences in negative affect or anxiety. Genital–subjective sexual arousal concordance was significantly positive for the asexual women and non-significant for the other three groups, suggesting higher levels of interoceptive awareness among asexuals.

[2] See the Glossary at the end of the book for a presentation of the key concepts used in this chapter (highlighted in bold on first mention).

[3] See: http://www.asexuality.org/home/overview.html (all websites cited in this chapter have been consulted in the period September–December 2012).

[4] From: http://www.asexuality.org/home/overview.html

[5] See: http://www.asexuality.org/home/overview.html

[6] The goal of Study no 1 was to examine relationship characteristics, frequency of sexual behaviours, sexual difficulties and distress, psychopathology, interpersonal functioning, and alexithymia in 187 asexuals recruited from AVEN. Asexual men ($n = 54$) and women ($n = 133$) completed validated questionnaires online. Study no 2 was designed to expand upon these quantitative findings with 15 asexuals from Study no 1 through in-depth telephone interviews.

[7] The scale was created by Dr Alfred Kinsey in his attempt to chart the level of an individual's sexual orientation over time. Kinsey evaluated degree of hetero- and homosexuality on a scale of 0 to 6, with 0 being exclusively heterosexual and 6 being exclusively homosexual. In the Kinsey Reports of 1948 and 1953, a separate category of 'X' was created for those with 'no socio-sexual contacts or reactions'. Based on his findings, Kinsey argued that very few people are exclusively oriented to one type of sexuality; he found numerous examples in between.

[8] The NSFG gathers information on family life, marriage and divorce, pregnancy, infertility, use of contraception, and men's and women's health. The survey results are used by the US Department of Health and Human Services and others to plan health services and health education programmes, and to do statistical studies of families, fertility and health. See: http://www.cdc.gov/nchs/nsfg.htm

[9] A nuclear family may be defined as a family consisting of a mother, father and their biological or adoptive children.

[10] HSDD is considered a sexual dysfunction and is characterised as a lack or absence of sexual fantasies and desire for sexual activity, as judged by a clinician.

[11] See: http://www.asexuality.org/home/

[12] See: http://www.asexuality.org/home/general.html and http://www.asexuality.org/home/family.html

[13] See: http://www.asexualawarenessweek.com/

[14] See: http://www.facebook.com/notes/asexual-awareness-week/results-of-the-asexual-community-census-2011/208581089214485?ref=nf

---

References

Berkey, B.R., Perelman-Hall, T. and Kurdek, L.A. (1990) 'The multidimensional scale of sexuality', *Journal of Homosexuality*, vol 19, no 4, pp 67–87.

Bogaert, A.F. (2004) 'Asexuality: prevalence and associated factors in a national probability sample', *Journal of Sex Research*, vol 41, no 3, pp 279–87.

Bogaert, A.F. (2006) 'Toward a conceptual understanding of asexuality', *Review of General Psychology*, vol 10, no 3, pp 241–50.

Bogaert, A.F. (2012) *Understanding asexuality*, Plymouth: Rowman and Littlefield Publishers.

Brotto, L.A. and Yule, M.A. (2011) 'Physiological and subjective sexual arousal in self-identified asexual women', *Archives of Sexual Behavior*, vol 40, no 4, pp 699–712. Available at: http://www.springerlink.com/content/th33mg9r647tj2v8/fulltext.pdf

Brotto, L.A., Knudson, G., Inskip, J., Rhodes, K. and Erskine, Y. (2010) 'Asexuality: a mixed methods approach', *Archives of Sexual Behavior*, vol 39, no 3, pp 599–618.

Caplan, P. (1987) 'The cultural construction of sexuality (introduction)', in P. Caplan (ed) *The cultural construction of sexuality*, London: Tavistock.

Carlat, D.J., Camargo, C.A., Jr. and Herzog, D.B. (1997) 'Eating disorders in males: a report on 135 patients', *American Journal of Psychiatry*, vol 154, no 8, pp 1127–32.

Carrigan, M. (2011) 'There's more to life than just sex? Difference and commonality within the asexual community', *Sexualities*, vol 14, no 4, pp 462–78.

Cerankowski, K.J. and Milks, M. (2010) 'New orientations: asexuality and its implications for theory and practice', *Feminist Studies*, vol 36, no 3, pp 650–64.

Davies, P. (1992) 'The role of disclosure in coming out among gay men', in K. Plummer (ed) *Modern homosexualities: fragments of lesbian and gay experience*, London and New York, NY: Routledge, pp 75–83.

DeLuzio Chasin, C.J (2011) 'Theoretical issues in the study of asexuality', *Archives of Sexual Behavior*, vol 40, no 4, pp 713–23.

Fracher, J.C. and Kimmel, M.S. (2005) 'Hard issues and soft spots: counseling men about sexuality', in M.S. Kimmel (ed) *The gender of desire. Essays on male sexuality*, New York, NY: Free Press, pp 139–48.

Freeman, T., Jadva, V., Kramer, W. and Golombok, S. (2009) 'Gamete donation: parents' experiences of searching for their child's donor siblings and donor', *Human Reproduction*, vol 24, no 3, pp 505-16.

Giddens A. (1992) *The transformation of intimacy: Sexuality, love and eroticism in modern societies*, Cambridge: Polity Press.

Golombok, S., MacCallum, F., Goodman, E. and Rutter, M. (2002) 'Families with children conceived by donor insemination: a follow-up at age twelve', *Child Development*, vol 73, no 3, pp 952–68.

Haefner, C. (2011) 'Asexual scripts: a grounded theory inquiry into the intrapsychic scripts asexuals use to negotiate romantic relationships', PhD dissertation, Institute of Transpersonal Psychology, Palo Alto, California. Available at: http://gradworks.umi.com/3457969.pdf

Jackson, S. and Scott, S. (2010) *Theorizing sexuality*, London: Open University Press.

Jenness, V. (1992) 'Coming out: lesbian identities and the categorization problem', in K. Plummer (ed) *Modern homosexualities: fragments of lesbian and gay experience*, London and New York, NY: Routledge, pp 65–74.

Johnson, M.T. (1977) 'Asexual and autoerotic women: two invisible groups', in H.L. Gorchros and J.S. Gochros (eds) *The sexually oppressed*, New York, NY: Association Press, pp 96–109.

Johnson, W.R. and Johnson, J.A. (1963) *Human sex and sex education*, Philadelphia, PA: Lea and Febiger.

Kim, E. (2010) 'How much sex is healthy? The pleasures of asexuality', in J.M. Metzl and A. Kirkland (eds) *Against health: how health became the new morality*, New York, NY: New York University Press, pp 157–69.

Kindregan, C.P., Jr. (2006) 'The new parentage: of families, sex, and asexual choices', Paper 31, Suffolk University Law School Faculty Publications. Available at: http://lsr.nellco.org/suffolk_fp/31

Kinsey, A., Pomeroy, W. and Martin, C. (1948) *Sexual behaviour in the human male*, Philadelphia, PA: W.B. Saunders.

Kinsey, A., Pomeroy, W., Martin, C. and Gebhard, P. (1953) *Sexual behaviour in the human female*, Philadelphia, PA: W.B. Saunders.

Lorber, J. (1994) *Paradoxes of gender*, New Haven, CT, and London: Yale University Press.

Markens, S. (2007) *Surrogate motherhood and the politics of reproduction*, Berkeley, CA: University of California Press.

Melby, T. (2005) 'Asexuality gets more attention, but is it a sexual orientation?', *Contemporary Sexuality*, vol 39, no 11, pp 1–5.

Miller, R. and Perlman, D. (2008) *Intimate relationships* (5th edn), New York, NY: McGraw Hill.

Nurius, P.S. (1983) 'Mental health implications of sexual orientation', *The Journal of Sex Research*, vol 19, no 2, pp 119–36.

Poston, D.L. and Baumle, A.K. (2010) 'Patterns of asexuality in the United States', *Demographic Research*, vol 23, pp 509–30. Available at: http://www.demographic-research.org/Volumes/Vol23/18/23-18.pdf

---

Prause, N. and Graham, C.A. (2007) 'Asexuality: classification and characterization', *Archives of Sexual Behavior*, vol 36, no 3, pp 341–56. Available at: http://www.kinseyinstitute.org/publications/PDF/PrauseGrahamPDF.pdf

Przybylo, E. (2011) 'Crisis and safety: the asexual in sexusociety', *Sexualities*, vol 14, no 4, pp 444–61. Available at: http://sexualities.sagepub.com/content/14/4/444.full.pdf+html

Rothblum, E.D. and Brehony, K.A. (1993) 'Why focus on romantic but asexual relationships among lesbians?', in E.D. Rothblum and K.A. Brehony (eds) *Boston marriages: romantic but asexual relationships among contemporary lesbians*, Boston, MA: The University of Massachusetts Press, pp 3–14.

Scheib, J.E., Riordan, M. and Rubin, S. (2003) 'Choosing identity-release sperm donors: the parents' perspective 13–18 years later', *Human Reproduction*, vol 18, no 5, pp 1115–27.

Scheib, J.E., Riordan, M. and Rubin, S. (2005) 'Adolescents with open-identity sperm donors: reports from 12–17 year olds', *Human Reproduction*, vol 20, no 1, pp 239–52.

Scherrer, K. (2008) 'Coming to an asexual identity: negotiating identity, negotiating desire', *Sexualities*, vol 11, no 5, pp 621–41.

Sell, R.L. (1996) 'The sell assessment of sexual orientation: background and scoring', *Journal of Gay, Lesbian, & Bisexual Identity*, vol 1, no 4, pp 295–310.

Storms, M.D. (1980) 'Theories of sexual orientation', *Journal of Personality and Social Psychology*, vol 38, no 5, pp 783–92.

Strong, B., Yarber, W.L., Sayad, B. and De Vault, C. (2008) *Human sexuality: diversity in contemporary America* (6th edn), New York, NY: McGraw-Hill.

Teman, E. (2011) 'Reflections on surrogate motherhood and the politics of reproduction', *Sociological Forum*, vol 26, no 1, pp 199–201.

Wellings, K. (1994) *Sexual behaviour in Britain: the national survey of sexual attitudes and lifestyles*, London: Penguin Books.

CHAPTER TWO

Childfree women and men: living without children

The term 'childfree'

The term *childfree* describes women and men who have made a personal decision not to have children. Childfree people define themselves as:

> adults who all share at least one common desire: we do not wish to have children of our own. We are teachers, doctors, business owners, authors, computer experts – you name it. We choose to call ourselves 'childfree' rather than 'childless', because we feel the term 'childless' implies that we're missing something we want – and we aren't.[1]

As we will see later on, the choice to remain childfree is growing: more and more women and men are choosing not to bear or rear children. In recent years, the declining birth rate in developed countries, including the US and many EU countries, has been attributed to couples, or at least women of child-bearing age, postponing and/or even eventually deciding against having children. In almost all European countries, total fertility rates (ie the average number of children that would be born to a woman over her lifetime) are below replacement levels (the 2.1 that is needed to maintain a stable population). Clearly, the increase in the number of couples remaining voluntarily childless is directly related to the long-term fertility decline in developed economies. But demographers and sociologists now predict that in the near future, around 20% of women in Europe and other relatively affluent countries will remain childless.

Childlessness itself is not a new phenomenon. However, if we compare the past to the present, significant differences emerge. As Hakim (2000) notes, childlessness in the past was due primarily to extreme poverty and poor nutrition, or to low marriage rates resulting from wars or emigration. That correlation is no longer relevant for Europe or the US. Although the trend towards lower fertility in Western nations began in the late 18th century (Degler, 1980), it fell steeply after the

Baby Boom, 'second-wave' feminism[2] and the economic recession of the 1970s. The cultural revolution of the late 1960s and 1970s (which was itself fuelled by a post-war prosperity that allowed people to give greater attention to non-material concerns; see Inglehart, 1977) played a key role in reconfiguring men's and women's views of marriage and family life. For the first time in history, women had access to reliable methods of contraception that they could control, with or without a partner's cooperation. The childfree movement really exploded in the 1970s, with numerous 'childless by choice' organisations springing up and issuing literature advocating the childfree lifestyle.

Research on childfree women and men

The principal database for the study of the decision to remain childfree is the United Nations-coordinated series of Family and Fertility Surveys (FFS) carried out in the mid-1990s across Western and Eastern Europe.[3] Analyses based on that series of surveys confirm the heterogeneity of that population (see next section). Childfree women and men are now a very diverse group, and childlessness among healthy, sexually active individuals living in relative prosperity is a different, more complex phenomenon (see next section for details). Indeed, research indicates that individuals and couples arrive at the decision for a combination of economic, social and emotional reasons. For example, a study by Tanturri and Mencarini on childlessness in Italy demonstrates the extreme variability of **life courses** among people who remain childless (Tanturri and Mencarini, 2008). The study by Tanturri and Mencarini shows that it is not easy to define the elements that constitute the childfree condition. Some people are childless for involuntary reasons, while others opt not to have children. The former implies the desire to have children but the inability to do so, either for financial or biological reasons. The latter, however, is a far more positive attitude, reflecting a desired condition and implying a sense of emancipation – a preference for childlessness as a positive state of affairs.

Given the heterogeneity among the childfree population, recent scholarship has aimed at identifying the characteristics of different groups of voluntarily childless people, as did a project conducted by the Economic and Social Research Council (ESRC) (Hakim, 2003), which identified two groups of childless people:[4]

- the *voluntary* childfree: childless people who definitely never wanted a pregnancy or children of their own, ever – they are consistently negative on all questions about children; and

- the *uncertain* childless: childless people who gave an uncertain or ambivalent reply on at least one question concerning the desire to have children.

Even here, a subjective element has to be taken into account. For example, while couples or individuals who have lived happily without children may prefer to describe themselves as 'childless by choice', others who wanted children, and struggled with infertility, may also eventually come to describe themselves as 'childfree'. The complexity in situations and motivations of the voluntarily childless makes it difficult to perform research in the field; a review of the existing scholarship finds mixed and sometimes conflicting results. This makes reliance on surveys that ask predictive questions problematic. European polls of whether young women intend to remain childless have consistently reported figures indicating a higher future preference for children than actual fertility rates confirm, revealing an apparent desire to conform to 'traditional family norms' (Rowland, 2007; Schwarz, 2007; Basten, 2009). It is also difficult to synthesise the existing literature on the trend of voluntary childlessness because of widely differing operational definitions and data sources (Basten, 2009; Chancey and Dumais, 2009).

In addition, much of the research on childlessness has used in-depth interview or case study designs (Hakim, 2000). Respondents have been generally recruited through either snowball samples or media campaigns, and their representativeness is questionable. For example, the sample of voluntary childlessness in Britain reported in McAllister and Clarke (1998) consisted of 30 women plus nine of their male partners. Another study conducted by Gillespie (2003) was based on interviews with 25 voluntarily childless women. The book by Lunneborg (1999) on childfree men – the first book to explore the motives and consequences of voluntary childlessness from a man's perspective – was based on in-depth interviews with 30 American and British men who were childless. The participants lived in America or Britain, with 28 being Caucasian; one was from Iran and the other was from Japan. They were a convenience sample with ages ranging from 27 to 56 years old.

Existing research has however underlined some interesting trends. To begin with, we now have some knowledge of the numbers of women and men who are childfree. In 2003, a US Census study found that a record 19% of US women aged 40–44 did not have children (compared with 10% in 1976). In 2004, another US Census study found that 18.4% of women aged 35–44 were childless. As Bloom and Pebley (1982) show, some analysts predict that as much as 30% of recent cohorts of American women will remain permanently childless. Moreover, estimates show signs of increase (Basten, 2009). A meta-analysis based on a series of studies estimating the rates of voluntary childlessness in the US within that population estimated that voluntary childlessness ranged between 1.6% and 4.5% in the 1970s, 1.8% and 6.4% in the 80s, and 7% during the period 1988 and 1994 (Mosher and Bachrach, 1982; Veevers, 1982; Heaton et al, 1999; Chancey and Dumais, 2009). Similar figures are reported for Europe. Hakim's (2003) study on childlessness in Europe shows that, focusing on people aged 20–39 years, voluntary childlessness is below 10% of men and women in all countries except Belgium and Austria, where 14% and 10% of men, respectively, are certain that they do not want children. In Slovenia and Latvia, voluntary childlessness falls to less than 1% of men and women. The proportion of uncertain childless is even more variable, ranging from nothing in Austria and 1% of men and women in Belgium, to 11% of women and 19% of men in Germany, and 5% of women and 18% of men in Poland. The contrasts between Poland and Hungary, and between Austria and Germany, are the focus of particular attention in the analyses. In Britain, using the National Child Development Study (NCDS)[5] and the British Cohort Study (BCS),[6] we find 7–8% voluntary childlessness at age 42, and 12% voluntary childlessness at age 30. The childless group that is uncertain or ambivalent about (not) having children is much larger: 12% of women and 21% of men at age 42, but one-third of women and almost half of men at age 30. The research group also identified a group of parents who could be classified as reluctant, or regretful, parents: 12% of women and 6% of men at age 42 (Hakim, 2003).

Overall, researchers have found that both men and women in childfree couples are better educated and more likely to be employed in professional and management occupations, to earn relatively high incomes, to live in urban areas, to be less religious, to subscribe to less traditional **gender roles**, and to be less conventional (see, among others, Baber and Dreyer, 1986; Heaton et al, 1992; Mosher et al, 1992; DeOllos and Kapinus, 2002; Biddlecom and Martin, 2006; Cwikel et al, 2006; Keizer et al, 2008; Kneale and Joshi, 2008). Indeed, a woman's education is the most important determinant of the likelihood of her reproducing. The higher her education, the less likely she is to bear children. For example, a study based on the Spanish FFS of 1995, which used event history models (Martín-García, 2009), found that young women who want to be childfree or end up being childless stay in school for a longer period of time and postpone forming domestic unions, while those with strong family/fertility intentions accelerate these processes.

Moreover, gender balance seems to be connected with the childfree attitude. The childfree couples studied by Veevers (1980) had unusually egalitarian relationships. Burgwyn (1981), too, cites voluntarily childless couples as usually having more egalitarian relationships, including non-traditional sex roles and the sharing of leadership and finances. Findings from these two studies support that theory. First, involuntarily childless couples had more egalitarian relationships than parents; second, no matter how egalitarian a couple's relationship was before the first child's birth, after the first child's birth, familial roles tended to move in a more traditional direction.

While much attention has been paid to the childfree orientation from a woman's point of view, men are often seen as playing a secondary role in the decision, and as ready to accept whatever their partner decides. Yet, voluntary childlessness is generally higher among men than among women, in all countries. Despite the fact that childbearing generally has a bigger impact on women's lives, women seem to be rather more keen to have children – although they also seem to be most likely to regret it. In the previously cited book by Lunneborg (1999), interviews indicated that there were two primary types of decision-makers in regard to reproduction. The author termed the first type as the 'articulator', a man who knew without a doubt that he did not want children. The second type was the 'postponer', who was a male who kept putting off the decision to reproduce until it was too late. Some of the reasons the men gave for not reproducing were personal development, work and money, and avoiding stress.

The desire to have children is generally seen as a positive characteristic. Consequently, childless adults are often regarded as defective or less caring. For example, Callan (1986) examined the perceptions of parents and the voluntarily and involuntarily childfree via a multidimensional scaling analysis. In Callan's study, 45 participants (24 single and 21 married male and female students) were asked to rate their perceptions of 16 fictitious fertility-status persons. The results of the study indicated that individuals were perceived differently based on their fertility status. The more children an individual was reported as having, the more likely respondents were to rate them positively. The voluntary childfree and one-child parents were judged least favourably. Callan (1986) concluded that individuals are perceived as disadvantaged if they do not have children or families of the 'right' size.

Other research confirms the probability that voluntarily childfree people will be perceived negatively. Two studies based on experiments conducted by Jamison, Franzini and Kaplan (1979) found that people who remain voluntarily childfree are perceived as less sensitive, loving and well-adjusted. Experiment 1 examined the attitudes of 156 undergraduates, 29 high school students and 32 adult school students towards a hypothetical childfree woman who opted for sterilisation. The childfree woman was seen as an atypical American woman: less sensitive and loving, and more likely to be active in women's liberation. Also, she was rated as less happy, less well-adjusted and less likely to be content at age 65. She was also seen as significantly different in several important ways from an otherwise identically described parent. In the second experiment, 116 undergraduates were given brief descriptions of two married men and two married women. The descriptions of all four hypothetical individuals alternated so that in each set of descriptions, one had two children, one was childfree and no mention of children was made for the other two. In 50% of the cases, the woman was voluntarily childfree (and had surgery to prevent pregnancy); in the other 50%, it was the man. Respondents described the woman with no children as more selfish and more atypical than the mother of two, while the woman who was described as a mother was rated as happier and better adjusted. Perceptions of differences among the fictional men were also quite striking. The childfree husband was perceived as significantly more selfish and less typical than the father of two, as well as less well-adjusted, less sensitive, less loving and less fulfilled. Moreover, the results of these experiments indicated that while married men who opt not to have children may be negatively stereotyped, even less desirable traits were ascribed to a sterilised childfree woman. The data also indicate that non-sterilised men and women are perceived differently when they are childfree and choose to remain so. Other studies have yielded similar results: the voluntarily childfree are stigmatised and may even face pressure to alter their choice (Mueller and Yoder, 1997). Based on in-depth interviews with 24 voluntarily childless women and men and a focus group that included seven of the interviewed individuals, the study by Park (2002) found that individuals who choose not to be parents are viewed in terms of negative stereotypes and experience social pressures to alter or justify their status.

In most parts of the world, there is a commonly held belief that all capable couples should have children, and children are portrayed as a requirement of adulthood. This belief has contributed to the development of a pro-natalist ideology that having children is good. Common and widely held pro-natalist stereotypes and norms include the following: 'All capable couples should have children'; 'Having children is good'; 'A couple's (woman's; man's) life cannot possibly be complete without children'; and 'Couples (women; men) with children are happier than childfree couples'. Moreover, women who say that they do not want children face even more prejudicial beliefs, such as: 'Women are made to be wives and mothers'; 'Women are fulfilled when they become mothers'; 'Your biological clock is ticking'; 'You don't know what you're doing; you'll change your mind eventually'; and 'You will regret it later'. The pro-natalist attitude is transmitted to children through **socialisation**. The media, in particular, assists in contributing to the stigmatisation and negative stereotypes of the voluntarily childfree. Sass (2004) notes, however, that the childless by choice subculture has received some minimal exposure in magazines, but has been largely overlooked by the more popular and highly visible media (TV, radio, movies, newspapers).

However, it seems that acceptance of voluntary childlessness is increasing. For example, within a relatively short period of 30 years, public acceptance of voluntary childlessness has increased enormously in the Netherlands (Den Bandt, 1980). Based on data from 13 waves of the cross-sectional[7] survey Cultural Change in the Netherlands[8] (CCN, 1965–96), the study by Noordhuizen, de Graaf and Sieben (2010) found that between 1965 and 1980, the change was primarily due to intra-cohort (period) effects, whereas cohort replacement has become more important since 1980. Moreover, church attendance – rather than religiosity or religious socialisation – turned out to be the most important variable in determining negative views of childfree couples. Low levels of income and education also negatively affect the acceptance of voluntary childlessness.

Finally, the already-mentioned study by Gillespie (2003), which drew on interviews with 25 voluntarily childless women, discusses the ways in which childfree women represent a fundamental and radical rejection of motherhood and the activities associated with it (see also Kelly, 2009). The article concludes by considering how to recast understandings of feminine identity away from a mother-centred focus.

Reasons to be childfree

The childfree movement is quite diverse; the childfree population runs the gamut from highly educated professionals to poor people struggling to make a living. As said in the previous section, there are a wide range of reasons why adults choose not to have children, which vary from a desire to avoid passing on negative genetic traits to a dislike of children. In addition, as more and more women are entering the workforce, pursuing careers and empowering themselves, traditional motherhood holds less appeal for some.

Research indicates (see, for example, Silka and Kiesler, 1977; Veevers, 1980, 1982; Houseknecht, 1983; Somers, 1993; Heaton, Jacobson, and Holland, 1999; McCallister and Clarke, 1999; Park, 2005; Chancey and Dumais, 2009, Gobbi, 2011) that couples arrive at this decision for a combination of economic, social and emotional factors, including:

- Dislike of children/lack of interest in children.
- Belief that one is too old to have children.
- Fear that a child may reduce personal freedom, personal well-being, **independence** (from either a personal or an economic point of view) or one's standard of living. Childfree couples have more time each day for working extra hours, with time left over for extracurricular activities or career orientation.
- Fear that the couple relationship may be negatively affected, and/ or fear that sexual activity may decline. The stress of child-rearing may damage some marriages, and the relationship simply cannot survive the stress. This is especially true when a pregnancy is not planned or when partners disagree about child-rearing strategies. For example, a couple's time together is never the same once a child enters the home. Dates have to be planned, babysitters arranged and dinnertime conversations become baby-focused. Concerning sexual activity, there is often not enough energy for sex, not to mention the fact that many couples allow their child to sleep in their bedroom for the first couple of years following the birth.
- Existing or possible health problems, including genetic disorders.
- Fear about the physical consequences of pregnancy, the childbirth experience and recovery. For example, fears about weight gain, stretch marks, morning sickness, pregnancy pain, delivery pain, post-partum depression, the erosion of physical desirability and so on.
- Lack of money, cost and lack of access to support networks and resources.
- Belief that one can make a greater contribution to society through one's work than through having children.
- Perceived or actual incapacity to be a responsible and patient parent.
- Belief that it is wrong to intentionally have a child when there are so many children available for adoption.
- Concern regarding environmental impacts such as overpopulation, pollution and resource scarcity.
- Anti-natalism – the belief in a negative, competitive, declining condition of the world and culture (eg global warming effects, war

or famine) and the wish to spare a potential child from those negative conditions and from the suffering of life.

A research study conducted by the Childless by Choice Project,[9] based on 171 self-selected voluntarily childless/childfree individuals (single, partnered and married) living in the US and Canada, shows that the top six motives indicated are: (1) 'I love our life, our relationship, as it is, and having a child won't enhance it'; (2) 'I value freedom and independence'; (3) 'I do not want to take on the responsibility of raising a child'; (4) 'I have no desire to have a child, no maternal/paternal instinct'; (5) 'I want to accomplish/experience things in life that would be difficult to do if I was a parent'; and (6) 'I want to focus my time and energy on my own interests, needs or goals'.

The childfree movement

The childfree movement is a grassroots social movement advocating childlessness by choice. The movement was started during the 1970s. While people have been opting not to have children for centuries, the childfree movement really exploded in the 1970s, with numerous 'childless by choice' organisations springing up and creating various publications talking about the childfree lifestyle. Two of the most notable childfree organisations that were established during the 1970s and the 1980s are the National Organization for Non-Parents[10] and No Kidding![11]

There is also a growing movement across the blogosphere of people who have chosen to remain childless. Contributors describe the social discrimination they face as a result of their decision not to have children. One Internet-based group, No Children by Choice, aims to 'celebrate the unconventional life choice of remaining childfree and to explore the resulting freedoms, difficulties, joys and challenges of that choice'.[12] The site specifically states that it does not engage in negativity or denigration of the 'traditional' family unit, saying:

> in fact, most of the people we hold dear have children, and they and their children are a big part of our life – but instead, through this site we strive to build upon the components of traditional families and then illustrate how the conscious choice to remain child-free can create a life of quality ... a family of two ... with no apologies ... with no regrets.

Another web-based group, Childfree by Choice WebRing,[13] aims at bringing together people who have made the decision to remain childfree and are satisfied with their lifestyle choice.

Notes

[1] From: http://www.childfree.net/ (all websites cited in this chapter have been consulted in the period September–December 2012).

[2] See the Glossary at the end of the book for a presentation of the key concepts used in this chapter (highlighted in bold on first mention).

[3] The FFS is a project conducted by the Population Activities Unit of the United Nations Economic Commission for Europe (UNECE). The FFS is a comparative survey regarding fertility and family that was held in 24 mainly European countries during the 1990s (see: http://www.unece.org/pau/ffs/ffs.html and http://www.rau.edu.uy/fcs/banco/DATA%20CENTER/fertility_and_family_survey.htm).

[4] The project, which covered the period December 2002–July 2003 and used 26 data sets for 25 countries (Norway, Sweden, Finland, the Netherlands, Belgium, France, Germany, Austria, Switzerland, Italy, Portugal, Spain, Greece, Estonia, Latvia, Lithuania, Poland, Hungary, Czech Republic, Slovenia, Bulgaria, Canada, the US and New Zealand), included two British cohort studies of people born in 1958 and 1970 (see: http://www.cls.ioe.ac.uk/page.aspx?&sitesectionid=59&sitesectiontitle=Welcome+to+the+British+birth+cohort+studies).

[5] The NCDS is a continuing longitudinal study that seeks to follow the lives of all those living in Great Britain who were born in one particular week in 1958. The aim of the study is to improve understanding of the factors affecting human development over the whole lifespan. The NCDS has gathered data from respondents on: child development from birth to early adolescence, child care, medical care, health, physical statistics, school readiness, home environment, educational progress, parental involvement, cognitive and social growth, family relationships, economic activity, income, training, and housing (see: http://www.esds.ac.uk/longitudinal/access/ncds/l33004.asp).

[6] The 1970 BCS (BCS70) follows the lives of more than 17,000 people born in England, Scotland and Wales in a single week of 1970. Over the course of cohort members' lives, the BCS70 has collected information on health, physical, educational and social development, and economic circumstances, among other factors. The BCS70 is managed by the Centre for Longitudinal

Studies (CLS) and funded by the ESRC. Since the birth survey in 1970, there have been seven 'sweeps' of all cohort members at ages 5, 10, 16, 26, 30, 34 and 38. The age 42 survey will continue until the end of 2012 (see: http://www.cls.ioe.ac.uk/).

[7] Cross-sectional surveys are used to gather information on a population at a single point in time. A cross-sectional survey studies a cross-section of the population at a specific moment or point in time. The term 'cross-section' indicates a wide sample of people of different ages, education, religion and so on (Ruspini, 2002).

[8] Cultural Change in the Netherlands is a longitudinal survey in which a representative sample of the Dutch population aged 16 and over is interviewed at regular intervals. The survey was carried out annually until 1998, since when it has been held every two years. The aim of the project is to construct opinion time series. The questionnaires used consist of selections of questions taken from earlier surveys, which are presented verbatim. The Social and Cultural Planning Office of the Netherlands (SCP) carried out the first survey in 1975; that survey was itself based on earlier surveys, the results of which had been stored in a databank, the Steinmetz Archive. The project is organised and funded by SCP, a Dutch government agency, whose task is to describe the status of welfare in the Netherlands and to advise the government on its welfare policy. The survey samples are representative and generally comprise around 2,000 respondents (Peters, 2001).

[9] The Childless by Choice Project is a research project, a book (Scott, 2009) and a documentary that explores the motives and the decision-making processes behind the choice to remain childfree. The survey was conducted by Laura S. Scott from November 2004 to July 2006. Of the respondents, 121 (71%) were women and 50 (29%) were men. Participants were asked to rate 18 statements reflecting frequently cited motivations for remaining childless on a Likert scale from zero to five, to the degree to which they identified with that statement or the degree to which it applied to them in the course of their decision-making. A zero rating would indicate that the motive statement was not applicable or that the respondent did not identify at all with that statement. A higher number would indicate the relative degree to which the respondent identified with the statement, a rating of five indicating a very strong identification with the statement or an acknowledgment that it is, or was, a primary motivator in the decision to be childless/childfree (see: http://www.childlessbychoiceproject.com/ and http://www.childlessbychoiceproject.com/Childless_by_Choice_Survey.html).

[10] The National Organization for Non-Parents (NON) was begun in Palo Alto, California, US by Ellen Peck and Shirley Radl in 1972. NON was formed to advance the notion that people could choose not to have children. Changing its name to the National Alliance for Optional Parenthood, it continued into the early 1980s both as a support group for those making the decision to be childfree and an advocacy group fighting pro-natalism (attitudes/advertising/etc promoting or glorifying parenthood) (see: http://en.wikipedia.org/wiki/National_Alliance_for_Optional_Parenthood).

[11] No Kidding! is an all-volunteer, non-profit social club for adult couples and singles who, for whatever reason, have never had children. It was founded in 1984 in Vancouver, British Columbia, Canada. Today, it is active in New Zealand, Canada and the US. Its membership grew after it launched a website in the 1990s (see: http://www.nokidding.net/).

[12] From: http://nochildrenbychoice.com/

[13] See: http://hub.webring.org/hub/childfreebychoic

References

Baber, K.M. and Dreyer, A.S. (1986) 'Gender-role orientations in older child-free and expectant couples', *Sex Roles*, vol 14, nos 9/10, pp 501–12.

Basten, S. (2009) 'Voluntary childlessness and being childfree', The Future of Human Reproduction, Working Paper no 5, St. John's College, Oxford and Vienna Institute of Demography, June. Available at: http://www.spi.ox.ac.uk/fileadmin/documents/pdf/Childlessness_-_Number_5.pdf

Biddlecom, A. and Martin, S. (2006) 'Childless in America', *Contexts*, vol 5, no 4, p 54.

Bloom, D.E. and Pebley, A.R. (1982) 'Voluntary childlessness: a review of the evidence and implications', *Population Research and Policy Review*, vol 1, no 3, pp 203–24.

Burgwyn, D. (1981) *Marriage without children*, New York, NY: Harper.

Callan, V.J. (1986) 'Single women, voluntary childlessness and perceptions about life and marriage', *Journal of Biosocial Science*, vol 18, no 4, pp 479–87.

Chancey, L. and Dumais, S.A. (2009) 'Voluntary childlessness in marriage and family textbooks, 1950–2000', *Journal of Family History*, vol 34, no 2, pp 206–23.

Cwikel, J., Gramotnev, H. and Lee, C. (2006) 'Never-married childless women in Australia: health and social circumstances in older age', *Social Science and Medicine*, vol 62, no 8, pp 1991–2001.

Degler, C.N. (1980) *At odds: women and the family in America from the revolution to the present*, New York, NY: Oxford University Press.

Den Bandt, M.L. (1980) 'Voluntary childlessness in the Netherlands', *Journal of Family and Economic Issues*, vol 3, no 3, pp 329–349. Available at: https://springerlink3.metapress.com/content/v011312w14103411/resource-secured/?target=fulltext.pdfandsid=4mh5nvjiua3bz05ms10mskmrandsh=www.springerlink.com

DeOllos, I.Y. and Kapinus, C.A. (2002) 'Aging childless individuals and couples: suggestions for new directions in research', *Sociological Inquiry*, vol 72, no 1, pp 72–80.

Gillespie, R. (2003) 'Childfree and feminine: understanding the gender identity of voluntarily childless women', *Gender Society*, vol 17, no 1, pp 122–36.

Gobbi, P.E. (2011) 'A model of voluntary childlessness', Discussion Paper 2011-1, Département des Sciences Economiques, Louvain-la-Neuve, UCL Press. Available at: http://sites-final.uclouvain.be/econ/DP/IRES/2011001.pdf

Hakim, C. (2000) *Work–lifestyle choices in the 21st century: preference theory*, New York, NY: Oxford University Press.

Hakim, C. (2003) 'Childlessness in Europe', research report to the Economic and Social Research Council (ESRC) on the project funded by research grant RES-000-23-0074, London, LSE/ESRC.

Heaton, T.B., Jacobson, C.K. and Holland, K. (1999) 'Persistence and change in decisions to remain childless', *Journal of Marriage and the Family*, vol 61, no 2, pp 531–9.

Heaton, T.B., Jacobson, C.K. and Fu, X.N. (1992) 'Religiosity of married couples and childlessness', *Review of Religious Research*, vol 33, no 3, pp 244–55.

Houseknecht, S.K. (1983) 'Voluntary childlessness', in M.B. Sussman and S.K. Steinmetz (eds) *Handbook of marriage and the family*, New York, NY: Plenum Press, pp 369–95.

Inglehart, R. (1977) *The silent revolution: changing values and political styles among Western publics*, Princeton, NJ: Princeton University Press.

Jamison, P.H., Franzini, L.R. and Kaplan, R.M. (1979) 'Some assumed characteristics of voluntarily childfree women and men', *Psychology of Women Quarterly*, vol 4, no 2, pp 266–73.

Keizer, R., Dykstra, P.A. and Jansenm, M.D. (2008) 'Pathways into childlessness: evidence of gendered life course dynamics', *Journal of Biosocial Science*, vol 40, no 6, pp 863–78.

Kelly, M. (2009) 'Women's voluntary childlessness: a radical rejection of motherhood?', *Women's Studies Quarterly*, vol 37, nos 3/4, pp 157–72.

Kneale, D. and Joshi, H. (2008) 'Postponement and childlessness: evidence from two British cohorts', *Demographic Research*, vol 19, no 58, pp 1935–64.

Lunneborg, P.W. (1999) *The chosen lives of childfree men*, Westport, CT: Bergin and Garvey.

Martín-García, T. (2009) 'The effect of education on women's propensity to be childless in Spain: does the field of education matter?', Collegio Carlo Alberto Working Papers, no 114. Available at: http://www.carloalberto.org/assets/working-papers/no.114.pdf

McAllister, F., and Clarke, L. (1998) *Choosing childlessness*, London, Family Policy Studies Centre.

Mosher, W.D., and Bachrach, C.A. (1982) 'Childlessness in the United States: estimates from the National Survey of Family Growth', *Journal of Family Issues*, vol 3, no 4, pp 517-43.

Mosher, W.D., Williams, L.B. and Johnson D.P. (1992) 'Religion and fertility in the United States: new patterns', *Demography*, vol 29, no 2, pp 199–214.

Mueller, K.-A. and Yoder, J.D. (1997) 'Gendered norms for family size, employment, and occupation: are there personal costs for violating them?', *Sex Roles*, vol 36, nos 3-4, pp 207-20.

Noordhuizen, S., de Graaf, P. and Sieben, I. (2010) 'The public acceptance of voluntary childlessness in the Netherlands: from 20 to 90 per cent in 30 years'. Available at: http://www.springerlink.com/content/76575q745xn36m71/

Park, K. (2002) 'Stigma management among the voluntarily childless', *Sociological Perspectives*, vol 45, no 1, pp 21–45.

Park, K. (2005) 'Choosing childlessness: Weber's typology of action and motives of the voluntarily childless', *Sociological Inquiry*, vol 75, no 3, pp 372–402.

Peters, L. (2001) *Respondent panel and face-to-face interview compared. The 'Cultural Changes in the Netherlands', Survey 2000*, The Hague.

Rowland, D.T. (2007) 'Historical trends in childlessness', *Journal of Family Issues*, vol 28, no 10, pp 1311–37.

Ruspini, E. (2002) *Introduction to longitudinal research*, London and New York, NY: Routledge.

Sass, E. (2004) 'Re-constructing the image of the voluntarily childfree: an ethnographic exploration of media representation and the childless by choice', MA thesis, School of Mass Communications, College of Arts and Sciences, University of South Florida, 1 July.

Schwarz, K. (2007) *Childlessness in Germany: past and present. Lifestyles, contraception and parenthood: proceedings of a workshop*, The Hague: H. Moors, pp 241–50.

Scott, L.S. (2009) *Two is enough: a couple's guide to living childless by choice*, Berkeley, CA: Seal Press.

Silka, L. and Kiesler, S. (1977) 'Couples who choose to remain childless', *Family Planning Perspectives*, vol 9, no 1.

Somers, M.D. (1993) 'A comparison of voluntarily childfree adults and parents', *Journal of Marriage and the Family*, vol 55, no 3, pp 643–50.

Tanturri, M.L. and Mencarini, L. (2008) 'Childless or childfree? Paths to voluntary childlessness in Italy', *Population and Development Review*, vol 34, no 1, pp 51–77.

Veevers, J.E. (1980) *Childless by choice*, Toronto: Butterworth.

Veevers, J.E. (1982) 'Differential childlessness by color: a further examination', *Social Biology*, vol 29, nos 1/2, pp 180–6.

CHAPTER THREE

Couples together yet apart: 'I love you but do not want to live with you'

The term 'living apart together'

A *living apart together* (LAT) relationship describes a couple, of the same or different gender, who live together but do not share the same home. That is, the term refers to couples, heterosexual or homosexual, married or not, who have an ongoing self-defined couple relationship without cohabiting (Trost, 1998). Partners living in LAT relationships have one household each.

Levin (2004) has suggested that the dual-residence aspect of LAT couples distinguishes them from a **commuting (or commuter) marriage**,[1] where there is one main household and a second residence that is used when one partner is away. Distance also demarcates LATs from commuting marriages. LAT couples may either live near each other or far apart, while commuting couples typically spend time apart in order for both partners to pursue professional careers and have residences where each member of the couple works. Finally, LAT arrangements now encompass cohabiting gay, lesbian, transsexual and transgender partners, not just heterosexual married couples, and for that reason, Holmes (2007) uses the term 'distance relationship'. These relationships are also sometimes referred to as 'non-residential partnerships' (Castro-Martín et al, 2008).

The LAT relationship is not a new family form. In the past, however, they were far less common and almost invisible (Levin, 2004). Historically, for example, couples had to endure separation mostly when the husbands' work regularly took them away from home (notably, when men worked as railroad builders, seamen or in the mines). In those cases, due to long-term separation, women were literally left to take their migrant husbands' place as managers of the household.

Not surprisingly, many LAT couples maintain separate households for very different reasons. For example, if, historically, it was the man who left the family for a period of time, corporate businesses today offer a growing proportion of job transfers to women (see, eg, Anderson and

Spruill, 1993). Hence, there is now an increasing likelihood of women needing to live separately from their family for work-related reasons. The already-discussed cultural move towards more individualised decision-making processes, a shift from normative actions towards individual choice behaviours, may also be a factor in the increasing number of such couples (Giddens, 1991; Beck and Beck-Gernsheim, 2001; Cliquet, 2003). According to Levin (2004), the LAT seems to have the potential of becoming the third stage (after traditional marriages and commuting marriages) in the process of the social transformation of **intimacy**.

Starting from these premises, this chapter will try to answer the following questions: 'How have non-cohabiting relationships evolved in recent decades?'; 'Why do people enter into LATs?'; 'Is this a temporary or a long-lasting decision?'; and 'What do we know about the children of LAT couples?'

Research on living apart together couples

The phenomenon of LAT is not easy to measure but is increasingly discussed in the international sociological and demographic literature. However, because most social surveys focus on partners sharing the same household, LAT partnerships are generally ignored in the literature depending on such data. For example, LAT individuals would be classified as 'single' in conventional studies that focus on co-residential unions. In addition, as we will see in the fourth section, there has also been very little research on non-residential partnerships among lesbians and gay men.

Nonetheless, a number of studies have examined the incidence and demographic characteristics of those who live apart together, the understandings that they hold about their relationships and why they do not live together (see, among others, Levin and Trost, 1999; Bawin-Legros and Gauthier, 2001; Borell and Karlsson, 2002, 2003; Milan and Peters, 2003; de Jong Gierveld, 2004; Levin, 2004; Haskey, 2005; Haskey and Lewis, 2006; Roseneil, 2006; Coast, 2009; Duncan and Phillips, 2010). Indeed, for a variety of reasons, LAT relationships have generated a growing interest on the part of sociologists, demographers and even the media.

First, to begin with, a large number of couples in Europe and North America have chosen to make a commitment to each other with the agreement that they will live separately. It is estimated that there are some two million men and women in Great Britain who report having a partner who lives in another household (Haskey, 2005). Also, a recent study estimated that in Great Britain, about three in every 20 men and women between the ages of 16 and 59 are in a relationship best described as 'living apart together' (Ermisch and Murphy, 2007). These couples are thought to account for around 10% of adults in Britain, a figure that equates to over a quarter of all those not married or cohabiting. Although as many as 13% of British Social Attitudes Survey (BSA)[2] respondents aged 55–64 outside a co-residential partnership are living apart together (Duncan and Phillips, 2010; see also Haskey, 2005; Ermisch and Seidler, 2009), LAT relationships are particularly common in younger age groups, accounting for almost 40% of 18–34 year olds outside a co-residential relationship in the 2006 BSA. Similar figures are recorded for other countries in Northern Europe, including Belgium, France, Germany, the Netherlands, Norway and Sweden (Levin, 2004; Haskey, 2005). Research suggests similar or even higher rates in Southern Europe, although, here, LAT couples often remain in parental households (Duncan and Phillips, 2010): the phenomenon described as 'young adults who LAT with parents' (Billari et al, 2008). LAT with parents is defined as the situation in which young adults who reside with their parents spend a significant amount of that time living outside the parental household. The relevance of this phenomenon is documented for Italy, a country with one of the highest shares of young adults cohabiting with parents and with fundamental sub-national differences both on higher education provision and in the labour market situation (Billari et al, 2008). Finally, in Australia, Canada and in the US, representative surveys indicate that between 6% and 9% of the adult population has a partner who lives elsewhere (Milan and Peters, 2003; Strohm et al, 2010; Reimondos et al, 2011).

Second, LAT relationships also result when one or both partners lead independent lives in ways not seen in the past. This is because LAT relationships give partners economic, personal, psychological or emotional independence: LATs can have both an intimate relationship and retain their own autonomy. As Bella DePaulo (2012) notes, LAT relationships offer the possibility of arranging the optimum balance of time alone and time together. Moreover, LAT relationships seem to facilitate an egalitarian division of labour (Haskey and Lewis, 2006). The connection between autonomy and LAT couples is uncommon and still needs to be explored. **Independence** is a crucial issue, especially for women's well-being. Women's vulnerability to poverty seems to be directly related to the absence of economic opportunities and autonomy and a lack of access to economic resources, including credit, land ownership and inheritance. Money management is indeed a predictor for personal well-being. Research (Taylor et al, 2011) based on data from the British Household Panel Survey (BHPS),[3] shows that for both men and women, poor money management skills have significant and substantial psychological costs over and above those associated with low income or deprivation. For men, the effect is similar to that of being unemployed, while for women, it is similar to going through a divorce. In contrast, superior financial capability is associated with higher levels of psychological health. The results also suggest that improving people's financial management skills would have substantial effects on stress-related illnesses and the outcomes associated with such problems, and would therefore have lasting benefits for individuals and the wider economy. Furthermore, poor financial situation exacerbates the psychological costs associated with being divorced or unemployed and of having low income. An implication is that by improving financial capability, policymakers can reduce the psychological impacts of experiencing such life events.

Finally, as we will see in the next section, this phenomenon may be one of the most important manifestations of the 'personalisation' and 'flexibilisation' of relationships in late modernity (as described in the introductory chapter to this book). First, the LAT attitude is closely related to contemporaneity and globalisation. Global interconnectedness helps such relationships flourish, while also making it easier for couples separated by choice or by life circumstances to stay in touch. Regardless of reasons, information and communication technologies (ICTs) may be the most crucial factor in keeping a LAT (or a long-distance) relationship alive and flourishing. However, while email, text-messaging and social networks facilitate LAT relationships, communication between partners must nonetheless be frequent, meaningful and open.[4]

LATs arise from quite diverse origins and motivations. Various studies have found that LATs do not necessarily live apart because they are forced to do so. Rather – to various degrees – some partners do not live together even when it is possible for them to do so (Levin, 2004). For example, a study by de Jong Gierveld, de Valk and Blommensteijn (2001)[5] on the living arrangements of older persons and family support shows that LATs are increasingly common among elderly people in developed countries.

In order to grasp such flexibility and heterogeneity, an ongoing Economic and Social Research Council (ESRC)-funded project – involving the University of Bradford, Birbeck College, University of London and the National Centre for Social Research (NatCen) – on LAT relationships[6] aims at studying the broad context in which LAT configurations emerge, as well as the individual motivations and understandings of what it means to be part of a LAT partnership, what these relationships mean to the couples involved, and whether these couples represent a 'new family form' or reflect the expansion of the 'traditional' family structure. The research is multi-method and will use large-scale representative survey data, semi-structured interviews and in-depth psychosocial, bio-narrative interviews.

Reasons for living apart

People in LAT relationships choose the arrangement for a variety of reasons and in diverse circumstances: individual choice; employment conditions and location; mobility requirements; financial condition; and so on. A substantial proportion of LAT partners indicate external constraints, work or school locations as the primary reasons for maintaining separate households. But family obligations may also affect the decision. A LAT couple may not want to impact the lives of their children by moving to a new household if doing so may force their children to move away from friends or school. A LAT relationship may also come into being if one partner needs to move to another city and that would create occupational problems for the other partner. Other LAT couples decide to live apart because they do not feel 'ready' to cohabit: this shows how women and men are waiting longer to progress through their relationship instead of rushing into commitments such as living together and getting married (Régnier-Loilier et al, 2009). A final reason may be involvement in a divorce. Qualitative evidence also suggests that individuals who have gone through a divorce or a relationship breakdown, experiences that have left them particularly 'risk averse', are more likely to decide to live apart (de Jong Gierveld et al, 2001; de Jong Gierveld, 2004; Levin, 2004; Roseneil, 2006). Divorced men and women may feel that if they get married or live with another person, they might recreate an environment or the conditions that would lead to another divorce. Maintaining separate households allows individuals to 'have a place of their own' away from their partner. The new relationship gives couples the flexibility to be in relationships with other people and still fulfil their obligations to family and children.

Previous research suggests that the meaning of LAT relationships and the reasons for forming them, as well as future intentions, depends very much on the stage of the individual **life course** (Régnier-Loilier et al, 2009; Strohm et al, 2010). LAT relationships appear to be more provisional and involuntary among younger cohorts. The geographic location of places of work or study, as well as financial and housing factors, may constrain or prevent young people from moving into a joint residence with their partner. Also, young people living at home are less likely than their older counterparts to have acquired the financial ability to set up a residence with their partner (Castro-Martín et al, 2008).

Some young couples may intend to marry but live apart due to the constraints of school and the labour market (Levin and Trost, 1999). Others form non-residential partnerships as part of the dating process; typically, these unions involve less long-term commitment. For example, a recent study suggests that, in Spain, LAT relationships among women aged 20–34 are a preliminary stage of the courtship process, potentially leading to cohabitation (Castro-Martín et al, 2008).

Among heterosexual women and men and among lesbians, age decreases the chance of being in a LAT union compared to a co-residential union (marriage for heterosexual women and men, cohabitation for lesbians). This pattern in both the national and Californian samples is consistent with qualitative evidence that LAT relationships are a way for (young) people to balance a desire for intimacy with the pursuit of education, work or financial goals (Levin, 2004).

In later years, individuals may choose to live apart from their partners to facilitate contact with adult children from previous unions or to maintain privacy and autonomy (Borell and Karlsson, 2003; de Jong Gierveld, 2004). For many older couples, a LAT relationship may also be a way of avoiding complicated inheritance issues. In the Netherlands, according to estimates by Loozen and Steenhof (2004), among 30 to 60 year olds, there are 125,000 single people (either with or without children) who have entered into a LAT relationship with a partner. Among older people, this type of relationship is more popular: more than four out of 10 people over 40 and nearly seven out of 10 people over 50 with a LAT partner do not want to live with that partner at any point in the future. Almost half of all people currently living alone who want to continue living alone in the future list preserving their freedom as their main reason for wanting to do so. In that sense, LAT relationships are part of the general trend of the informalisation of relationships. More than one in 10 people who say that they prefer a LAT relationship are influenced in their decision-making by the fact that they have children from a previous relationship. Another 10% list bad experiences as an important reason. Nearly 75% of those entering into a LAT relationship have been involved in previous relationships (Loozen and Steenhof, 2004).

Another important theoretical question regarding LATs relates to the meaning of these partnerships and whether they are a transitory step taken before entering a live-in relationship, or whether they are a more permanent arrangement (Reimondos et al, 2011). Involuntary non-residential relationships may also be the result of caring responsibilities for children or elderly parents (Levin, 2004). While these circumstances prevent individuals from moving in together, the possibility to cohabit is there if and when circumstances change. Alternatively, LAT relationships can be more permanent arrangements that allow for intimacy but also autonomy and independence, and this appears to be particularly the case for older individuals (Levin, 2004). The German Socio-economic Panel (GSOEP)[7] provides the unique opportunity to study trends regarding LAT partnerships separately from singledom and cohabitation in Germany since 1992. The study includes both cross-sectional and **longitudinal** data. The results indicate: a substantial increase in LAT relationships between 1992 and 2006, particularly after mid-adulthood; that LAT women are as likely to live in a household with their children as they are to be single or cohabiting; that while LAT relationships are likely to end earlier than cohabiting ones, LAT partners report similar levels of life satisfaction; and that with increasing age, LAT couples are more likely to remain apart than to move in together. The results suggest that early LAT is mainly a type of partnership coming before co-residency, but later becomes a lifestyle of its own (Asendorp, 2008).

Invisible living apart together people?

The web presence of the LAT community is not particularly strong. We may cite only a very few examples, such as the Living Apart Together website (see: http://livingapart.org/). This is an online community that is open for the free exchange of information. LAT women and men are invited to become a part of the community by registering and joining the conversation.

This weak online presence is probably due to the fact that LAT relationships have only recently been recognised and accepted as a particular form of partnering. However, both lack of information and stigmatisation of such relationships remain problems.

On the one hand, as we have seen, LAT partnerships are often ignored in social surveys, which generally focus on partners sharing the same household. In addition, even when social scientists study them, some aspects of LAT culture are largely ignored. One first, interesting aspect is the (still unexplored) connection between lack of physical intimacy and communication. Current global interconnectedness may help LAT and long-distance relationships flourish, while also making it easier for couples separated by life circumstances or by choice to stay in touch. The increasing popularity of social networks (as described in the introductory chapter to this book, the Millennial generation are the first 'true' digital natives) also results in people from all around the world meeting online and forming relationships, sometimes not making physical contact for weeks or months while forging emotional relationships.[8]

Another crucial point is that there has been very little research on non-residential partnerships among lesbians and gay men. Although we have theory and data that provide insights about LAT relationships among lesbians and gay men, in fact, demographic research on same-sex LAT couples is even more limited by data availability than is research on heterosexual couples.

Some studies (eg Strohm et al, 2010) show that gay men are somewhat more likely than heterosexual men to be in LAT relationships. For heterosexuals and lesbians, LAT relationships are more common among younger people. Heterosexuals in LAT unions are less likely to expect to marry their partners, but more likely to say that couples should be emotionally dependent than are cohabiters. This may be linked to discrimination against homosexuals and opposition to homosexual marriage: for example, same-sex couples cannot marry and cannot adopt or foster children in many US states and European countries. These obstacles are likely to make non-residential partnerships more attractive to lesbians and gay men than to heterosexual women and men.

Homophobia may actually increase the desirability of forming a LAT relationship because non-residential partnerships keep sexuality more private than does moving in together (Peplau and Cochran, 1990; Steven and Murphy, 1998). Two other factors may contribute to a higher prevalence of non-residential unions among lesbians and gay men compared to heterosexuals. First, individuals' expectations that part of being a couple includes sharing a household may be much stronger for heterosexual unions than for same-sex unions.

Because lesbians and gay men are less likely than heterosexuals to express interest in having children (Gates et al, 2007), and because same-sex couples are less likely to have children (Black et al, 2000), sharing a residence may be a less salient feature of same-sex than heterosexual unions. Second, if LAT relationships facilitate an egalitarian division of labour (Haskey and Lewis, 2006), and if gay men and lesbians are more likely than heterosexual women and men to seek equality in their intimate relationships (Kurdek, 2005), then LAT unions may be more common among gay men and lesbians than among their heterosexual counterparts.

A study by Carpenter and Gates (2008) offers some insight on the prevalence and demographic correlates of LAT unions among self-identified lesbians and gay men in the US. Using data from the *2003 California LGBT Tobacco Use Survey*,[9] Carpenter and Gates (2008) found that 11% of lesbians and gay men aged 18 to 59 years old are in non-residential partnerships. These non-residential partnerships are of shorter duration than cohabiting unions, especially for lesbians. The results also show that lesbians in non-residential unions are younger than are lesbians who are living with their partner and also younger than their single counterparts, but among gay men, there is little or no difference in mean age by union status.

Notes

[1] See the Glossary at the end of the book for a presentation of the key concepts used in this chapter (highlighted in bold on first mention).

[2] The BSA is an annual survey that measures changes in social attitudes that has been charting changing values in Britain since 1983. Core-funded by the Sainsbury Family Charitable Trust, its findings are based on hour-long interviews with a sample of 3,600 people. The survey is designed to yield a representative sample of adults aged 18 and over. Two of the main purposes of the BSA series are to allow monitoring of patterns of continuity and change, and the examination of the relative rates at which attitudes change over time with respect to social issues. The subjects covered by the surveys are wide-ranging but include housing and home ownership, work and unemployment, health and social care, education, business and industry, social security and dependency, tax and spending, the welfare state, transport, environment and the countryside, constitutional reform, law and order, civil liberties, moral issues and sexual mores, racism and sexism, social inequality, religion, and politics and governance (see: http://www.esds.ac.uk/government/bsa/). (All websites cited in this chapter have been consulted in the period September–December 2012.)

[3] The BHPS was launched in 1991. The BHPS is being carried out by the Institute for Social and Economic Research (ISER) (incorporating the ESRC Research Centre on Micro-social Change) at the University of Essex. The main objective of the survey is to further the understanding of social and economic change at the individual and household level in Britain and to identify, model and forecast such changes, their causes and their consequences in relation to a range of socio-economic variables. It was designed as an annual survey of each adult (16+) member of a nationally representative sample of more than 5,500 households, making a total of approximately 10,200 individual interviews. Additional samples of 1,500 households in each of Scotland and Wales were added to the main sample in 1999, and in 2001, a sample of 2,000

households was added in Northern Ireland, making the panel suitable for UK-wide research (see: https://www.iser.essex.ac.uk/bhps).

[4] See: http://completewellbeing.com/article/long-distance-relationships/

[5] Data for this study are from the database of the Dynamics of Ageing project, initiated and executed by the Population Activities Unit of the Economic Commission for Europe in Geneva. The data consist of cross-nationally comparable microdata samples based on the 1990 round of population and housing censuses in countries of Europe and North America. In the paper, data about the following countries were presented: Finland, representing the Northern European countries; the United Kingdom of Great Britain and Northern Ireland, representing the Western European countries; Italy, representing Southern Europe; and Hungary, representing the European countries in transition.

[6] See: http://www.applied-social-research.brad.ac.uk/livingaparttogether/

[7] The GSOEP is a representative longitudinal survey of approximately 11,000 private households in the Federal Republic of Germany from 1984 to 2011 and Eastern German *Länder* from 1990 to 2011. The GSOEP is produced by the Deutsches Institut für Wirtschaftsforschung Berlin (DIW). Variables include household composition, occupations, employment, earnings, health and satisfaction indicators (see: http://www.eui.eu/Research/Library/ ResearchGuides/Economics/Statistics/DataPortal/GSOEP.aspx).

[8] See: http://completewellbeing.com/article/long-distance-relationships/

[9] In 2003-04, Field Research Corporation conducted a state-wide household survey of the Californian lesbian, gay, bisexual, and transgender (LGBT) population for the Tobacco Control Section (TCS), Department of Health Services (DHS). The purpose was to assess tobacco-related behaviours, attitudes, and knowledge within the LGBT population; identify disparities between the LGBT and general adult populations of the State; and explore possible explanations for the most important differences (see: http://www. cdph.ca.gov/programs/tobacco/Documents/CTCP-LGBTTobaccoStudy. pdf).

References

Anderson, E.A. and Spruill, J.W. (1993) 'The dual-career commuter family: a lifestyle on the move', *Marriage and Family Review*, vol 19, nos 1/2, pp 131–47. Available at: http://majorsmatter.net/family/Anderson.pdf

Asendorp, J.B. (2008) 'Living apart together: eine eigenständige Lebensform?', SOEPpapers no 78, DIW Berlin, the German Socio-Economic Panel (SOEP). Available at: http://ideas.repec.org/p/diw/diwsop/diw_sp78.html

Bawin-Legros, B. and Gauthier, A (2001) 'Regulation of intimacy and love semantics in couples living apart together', *International Review of Sociology*, vol 11, no 1, pp 39–46.

Beck, U. and Beck-Gernsheim, E. (2001) *Individualization. Institutionalized individualism and its social and political consequences*, London: Sage Publications.

Billari, F.C., Rosina, A., Ranaldi, R. and Romano, M.C. (2008) 'Young adults living apart and together (lat) with parents: a three-level analysis of the Italian case', *Regional Studies*, vol 42, no 5, pp 625–39.

Black, D., Gates, G., Sanders, S. and Taylor, L. (2000) 'Demographics of the gay and lesbian population in the United States: evidence from available systematic data sources', *Demography*, vol 27, no 2, pp 139–54.

Borell, K. and Karlsson, S.G. (2003) 'Reconceptualising intimacy and ageing: living apart together', in S. Arber, K. Davidson and J. Ginn (eds) *Gender and ageing: changing roles and relationships*, New York, NY: McGraw Hill, pp 47–62.

Carpenter, C. and Gates, G. (2008) 'Gay and lesbian partnership: evidence from California', *Demography*, vol 45, no 3, pp 573–90.

Castro-Martín, T., Domínguez-Folgueras, M. and Martín-García, T. (2008) 'Not truly partnerless: non-residential partnerships and retreat from marriage in Spain', *Demographic Research*, vol 18, no 16, pp 438–68.

Cliquet, R. (2003) 'Major trends affecting families in the new millennium. Western Europe and North America', in United Nations (ed) *Major trends affecting families. A background document*, prepared by the Programme on the Family, New York, NY: United Nations, pp 1–26. Available at: http://www.un.org/esa/socdev/family/Publications/mtcliquet.pdf and http://social.un.org/index/Family/Publications/MajorTrendsAffectingFamilies.aspx

Coast, E. (2009) 'Currently cohabiting: relationship attitudes, expectations and outcomes', in J. Stillwell, E. Coast and D. Kneale (eds) *Fertility, living arrangements, care and mobility: understanding population trends and processes*, Dordrecht: Springer. Available at: http://eprints. lse.ac.uk/23986/1/Currently_cohabiting_(LSERO).pdf

De Jong Gierveld, J. (2004) 'Remarriage, unmarried cohabitation, living apart together: partner relationships following bereavement or divorce', *Journal of Marriage and the Family*, vol 66, no 1, pp 236–43.

De Jong Gierveld, J., de Valk, H. and Blommensteijn, M. (2001) 'Living arrangements of older persons and family support in more developed countries'. Available at: http://www.un.org/esa/population/ publications/bulletin42_43/dejong_gierveld.pdf

DePaulo, B. (2012) 'A new American experiment', *Room for debate*, The New York Times, The Opinion Pages, February 13, http:// www.nytimes.com/roomfordebate/2012/02/12/the-advantages- and-disadvantages-of-living-alone/living-apart-and-together-the- optimum-balance

Duncan, S. and Phillips, M. (2010) 'People who live apart together (LATs) – how different are they?' . Available at: http://www.crfr. ac.uk/reports/slpresentations/Simon%20Duncan.pdf

Ermisch, J. and Murphy, M. (2007) *Changing household and family structures and complex living arrangements*, ESRC (Economic and Social Research Council).

Ermisch, J. and Seidler, T. (2009) 'Living apart together', in M. Brynin and J. Ermisch (eds) *Changing relationships*, Routledge: New York & London, Chapter 2, pp 29–44.

Gates, G., Badgett, L., Macomber, J. and Chambers, K (2007) *Adoption and foster care by lesbian and gay parents in the United States*, Washington, DC: The Urban Institute. Available at: http://www.urban.org/ publications/411437.html

Giddens, A. (1991) *Modernity and self-identity. Self and society in the late modern age*, Cambridge: Polity Press.

Haskey, J. (2005) 'Living arrangements in contemporary Britain: having a partner who usually lives elsewhere and living apart together (LAT)', *Population Trends*, vol 122, pp 35–45.

Haskey, J. and Lewis, J. (2006) 'Living-apart-together in Britain: context and meaning', *International Journal of Law in Context*, vol 2, no 1, pp 37–48.

Holmes, M. (2007) 'Couples living apart together', in G. Ritzer (ed) *Blackwell encyclopedia of sociology*, London: Blackwell. Available at: http:// www.blackwellreference.com/public/tocnode?id=g9781405124331_ yr2012_chunk_g97814051243319_ss1-142

Kurdek, L.A. (2005) 'What do we know about gay and lesbian couples?', *Current Directions in Psychological Science*, vol 14, no 5, pp 251-4.

Levin, I. (2004) 'Living apart together: a new family form', *Current Sociology*, vol 52, no 2, pp 223–40.

Levin, I. and Trost, J. (1999) 'Living apart together', *Community, Work and Family*, vol 2, no 3, pp 279–94.

Loozen, S. and Steenhof, L. (2004) 'Ruim 125 duizend personen met een l.a.t. relatie' ['Over 125,000 people in a partnership live apart'], *Statistics Netherlands Webmagazine*, 12 January. Available at: www.cbs.nl

Milan, A. and Peters, A. (2003) 'Couples living apart', *Canadian Social Trends*, Statistics Canada Catalogue, no 11-008, pp 2–6.

Peplau, L. and Cochran, S. (1990) 'A relationship perspective on homosexuality', in D. McWhirter, S. Sanders and J. Reinisch (eds) *Homosexuality/heterosexuality: concepts of sexual orientation*, New York, NY: Oxford University Press, pp 321–49.

Régnier-Loilier, A., Beaujouan, E. and Villeneuve-Gokalp, C. (2009) 'Neither single, nor in a couple: a study of living apart together in France', *Demographic Research*, vol 21, pp 75–108. Available at: http://www.demographic-research.org/Volumes/Vol21/4/21-4.pdf

Reimondos, A., Evans, A. and Gray, E. (2011) 'Living-apart-together (LAT) relationships in Australia', *Family Matters*, vol 87, pp 43–55. Available at: http://melbourneinstitute.com/downloads/hilda/Bibliography/Conference_Papers/Reimondos_LAT_TASA09.pdf

Roseneil, S. (2006) 'On not living with a partner: unpicking coupledom and cohabitation', *Sociological Research Online*, vol 11, no 3. Available at: http://www.socresonline.org.uk/11/3/roseneil.html

Steven, J. and Murphy, B. (1998) 'Gay and lesbian relationships in a changing social context', in C. Patterson and A. D'Augelli (eds) *Lesbian, gay, and bisexual identities in families: psychological perspectives*, New York, NY: Oxford University Press, pp 99–121.

Strohm, C., Selzer, J.A., Cochran, S.D. and Mays, V. (2010) '"Living apart together" relationships in the United States', *Demographic Research*, vol 21, no 7, pp 177–214. Available at: http://www.ncbi.nlm.nih.gov/pmc/articles/PMC3091814/

Taylor, M., Jenkins, S. and Sacker, A. (2011) 'Financial capability, income and psychological wellbeing', Institute for Social and Economic Research Working Paper Series, no 2011-18. Available at: http://www.iser.essex.ac.uk/publications/working-papers/iser/2011-18.pdf

Trost, J. (1998) 'LAT relationships now and in the future', in K. Matthijs and W.A. Dumon (eds) *The family: contemporary perspectives and challenges: Festschrift in honor of Wilfried Dumon*, Leuven: Leuven University Press, pp 209–20.

Section Two

Gender change and challenges to
traditional forms of parenthood

CHAPTER FOUR

Stay-at-home husbands and fathers

Stay-at-home men

A *stay-at-home husband* (also 'househusband') may be defined as a husband that chooses to stay at home instead of working at a career. A *stay-at-home father* (alternatively, 'stay-at-home dad', 'house dad', 'house-spouse') is a term used to describe a father who is the main carer of the children and is the homemaker of the household.

As we will see in the next section, the number of househusbands and stay-at-home fathers has been gradually increasing, especially in Western nations. Although the role is still subject to many **gender stereotypes**,[1] and men may have difficulties accessing parenting benefits, communities and services targeted at mothers, it is becoming more socially acceptable. The roles offer economic benefits to the family, and enable strong emotional development for the children. However, in some regions of the world, the stay-at-home husband/father remains culturally unacceptable.

Stay-at-home husbands and fathers are of interest to researchers and service providers for several reasons. To begin with, they are a testimony to the changes occurring in **gender identities**. Househusbands have broken with traditional gender role norms and, as a result, must carve out their own paternal and masculine identities within spaces traditionally considered feminine (Doucet, 2004, 2006). This is a challenge for social theory and social research. Home and private life have been significant in the formation of modern female identities (Giles, 2004). As seen in the introductory chapter to this book, the transformation from household artisan production to early industrial production was grounded in the creation of an outside-the-home male wage worker who was economically dependent on a boss, but also functioned as an independent economic provider for dependent wives and families. Consequentially, men became dependent on women's care and support. Employment has for a long time played a key role in the construction and reproduction of masculinity. For example, traditionally male jobs became a proving ground for masculinity, and organisational structures and practices provided the means to demonstrate one's virility (see, eg, Iacuone, 2005). Women's care and support in the household were seen as necessary pillars of that identity. Thus, househusbands are challenging the 'traditional' (modern) relationship between labour outside the home, production and masculinity.

However, studies on the impact of father involvement in childcare on later child outcomes confirm the importance of early paternal investment both in caring and in improving opportunities for women (see, among others, Pruett, 2000; Lamb, 2004; US Department of Health and Human Services, 2004; Doucet, 2006). The growing number of stay-at-home fathers and men's increased use of parental and family leave provide further evidence of the evolving role of men in the provision of childcare. This also suggests that paternal care of children has become an increasingly important childcare resource for families.

The social, educational, cultural and political implications that can be drawn from the increasing number of men who become househusbands and stay-at-home fathers, either by necessity or choice, deserves much more scientific attention. They do not represent any of the key 'alpha' masculinities (complicit, subordinate or hegemonic) detailed by Connell (1987, 1995) and Kimmel (1995, 1996; see also Ruspini, 2011a), but rather reflect processes 'of internal complexity and contradiction' as well as the 'dynamics' of changing and maturing masculinities (Connell, 2000, p 13). Father involvement is a multifaceted, complex and dynamic experience. Therefore, although fathers have many common experiences when parenting their children, they also face many unique challenges associated with their social background, their relationship with their own mothers and fathers, and changing social conditions, such as separation and divorce.

Starting from these premises, this chapter will try to answer a number of questions: 'What does it mean, today, to be a househusband?'; 'What leads these men to take on that role?'; 'Does this choice affect their sense of masculinity and, if so, how?'; and 'What are the pros and cons of this situation?'. Men who perform care work have chosen a work that is downgraded and de-professionalised, thus potentially creating low social esteem. This raises the question of how men who nevertheless opt for care can reconcile this transgression with the norms of hegemonic masculinity (Connell, 1995) and, consequently, if and how the gendered relations, norms and practices of care work are being transformed when men participate in these activities.

Research on stay-at-home husbands and fathers

While the changes in women's roles have been widely debated in the last 10 years (both in women's thinking and in that of men), those relating to men have been much less discussed. Moreover, despite the growing attention to male involvement in domestic labour, the literature on stay-at-home men is still limited. If research on stay-at-home masculinities and fatherhood has increased over the last several decades, research comparing the gender-typed characteristics and gender role attitudes of stay-at-home and employed fathers is still in its infancy (Fischer and Anderson, 2012).

Existing research has, however, underlined some interesting trends. First, although the number of stay-at-home dads still pales in comparison to women who make that choice, these numbers are growing. According to the US Bureau of the Census (Current Population Survey data),[2] in 1994, there were 76,000 stay-at-home dads out of a total of 4.5 million stay-at-home parents. Strikingly, that number just about doubled over the next decade: in 2008, an estimated 140,000 married fathers worked in the home as their children's primary carers while their wives worked outside of the home to provide for the family.[3] In the UK, data compiled by the Office for National Statistics show that in 2011, 62,000 men whose partners go out to work were classed as 'economically inactive', compared to just 21,000 in 1996. A survey from the insurance company Aviva[4] suggested that there could be 600,000 men, 6% of British fathers, in that role, a further rise from the Office for National Statistics figures, which recorded 192,000 British men as the primary carer for children in 2009 and 119,000 in 1993. The Australian Bureau of Statistics (ABS, 2006)[5] shows that in September 2003, some 47,500 fathers (or 29% of those who were not employed) stated that they did not want to work. Of the 1.7 million couple families with children aged 0–14 years in June 2003, there were 57,900 families (or 3.4%) where the father was not employed while the mother worked either full-time or part-time. A further 108,100 couples with children aged less than 15 years (or 6.3%) had neither parent working. Other empirical evidence from Statistics Canada based on data from the Labour Force Survey (LFS)[6] shows that in 2009, there were approximately 53,765 stay-at-home fathers in Canada, compared to 20,610 in 1976 (Hoffman, 2008). And while the number of stay-at-home mothers in mother–father families has decreased dramatically – from 1.5 million in 1976 to 436,995 in 2009 – the number of stay-at-home fathers has almost tripled since the mid-1970s. In 1976, stay-at-home fathers represented only 1% of all stay-at-home parents, while in 2009, 12% of the stay-at-home parents in Canadian mother–father families were men.

These trends seem to indicate that the number of stay-at-home men is likely to increase, and that might be at least partially a result of evolving attitudes about **gender roles** in parenting. As Edwards (2006) argues, masculinity is now less defined through work: the notion that a man's occupation is central to his identity is now in question. But there are also some other factors that may account for some of the increase. One is the impact of economic fluctuations on the employment prospects of men and fathers. Unemployment, combined with the rising costs of day care and preschool, make a stay-at-home parent more appealing to some families.

Another factor that may explain some of the increase is the growing phenomenon of the primary earner female partner (Sussman and Bonnell, 2006). One of the most dramatic transformations in the labour market in recent decades has been the growth in the labour force participation of married women. As a result, dual-earner, husband-and-wife families are quickly becoming the norm, shattering the image of the 'traditional' family in which the husband is the only and primary breadwinner. One notable corollary has been an increase in wives earning more than their husbands (Winkler, 1998). When families wish to have one parent at home while children are young, the decision about which parent stays at home has always been partly based on which partner has the highest salary, benefits and job security.

Of course, if more men (and their female partners) are open to the idea of fathers taking primary responsibility for household management, that also requires explanation. Among the most common reasons is that the wife may have, as we just said, a better job or pay packet and it is more feasible for him to leave his job than it is for her. Some men are also quite comfortable taking up the duties of a homemaker. The qualitative study by Rochlen et al (2008) found that most of the stay-at-home fathers in their sample really enjoyed staying at home with the children.[7] Also, Doucet and Merla (2007), in a study about the experiences of stay-at-home fathering in two countries (Canada and Belgium),[8] found that the desire to be the primary carer was most often listed as the reason for choosing to stay at home.

Some couples choose to have the father stay at home to undertake principal caring roles for children. The previously mentioned study by Rochlen et al (2008) emphasised two aspects of wanting to become a primary carer: both the mother and father believe that one parent should stay at home with the children rather than put them in day care; and both believe that the father is more suitable for the stay-at-home role. For other couples, circumstances such as unemployment or an inability to participate in the labour force (eg through disability) may necessitate the father staying at home.

Doucet's (2004) study of 70 stay-at-home fathers in Canada[9] found three dominant patterns that characterised the men's home–work balance. The first cluster involved fathers who had achieved financial and professional success and wanted to take a break from working and/or were seeking to move into another line of work once their children were in school. The overarching commonality among this group of fathers was that they seemed to have achieved their career goals and were looking for other forms of fulfilment, one of which was caring for their children as well as alternative work or leisure interests (eg travel, sports, writing). The second pattern was exhibited by men who were taking a break from working (on extended parental leave), were in transition between jobs or were planning to or were currently enrolled in college or university programmes for further education or training. The latter group also included men who had lost their jobs, who were debilitated as a result of a serious illness and who described themselves as having been stuck in dead-end jobs. A third group involved men who were working part-time, had flexible hours and could work from a home office, or were employees in a business owned by their wife or partner.

It is important to remember that stay-at-home men and fathers are not always unemployed and that the 'stay-at-home' period may be a temporary one. In another qualitative study of 118 primary carer Canadian fathers (Doucet, 2006), roughly half of the stay-at-home fathers were actually working to some extent – either part-time or with flexible hours from home.[10] Finally, a very recent study (Fischer and Anderson, 2012) of a group of stay-at-home ($n = 35$) and employed ($n = 49$) fathers shows that compared to employed fathers, stay-at-home fathers reported less traditional gender role attitudes. Wanting to be a stay-at-home father was rated the most important reason for staying at home. The more important the female partner was in influencing the decision to stay at home, the lower the levels of masculine characteristics and the more enjoyment men reported in being a stay-at-home father (see also Coltrane and Ishii-Kuntz, 1992; Greenstein, 1996). Fischer and Anderson (2012) conclude by saying that future research should focus on comparisons of paternal involvement among stay-at-home and other fathers, the reasons men decide to become stay-at-home fathers or not, and the factors that influence those reasons, such as their partners' attitudes and experiences with prejudice and discrimination.

Male carers, couples and children

As just seen, the reasons for the decision to become a stay-at-home husband may emerge when a couple decide to have a child. Many parents realise that parenting (father's and mother's) support is vital during the children's growing years.

A growing literature has led awareness of the importance of fathers to the development of their children (Coltrane, 1996; Allen and Daly, 2002; Lamb, 2004). That role seems to be especially important for children from disadvantaged backgrounds (Burgess, 2005). There is a substantial body of research literature documenting the positive benefits fathers bring to the lives of both their male and female children (see, eg, Snarey and Vaillant, 2002). A number of studies suggest that children of fathers who are involved, nurturing and playful develop better linguistic and cognitive capacities and experience better educational outcomes than the children of uninvolved fathers. Fathers also have an important role to play in their children's literacy development. Numerous studies find that an active and nurturing style of fathering is associated with better verbal skills, intellectual functioning and academic achievement among adolescents (Pruett, 2000; Lamb, 2004; Rosenberg and Bradford, 2006; Marsiglio and Roy, 2012). There is also evidence that schoolchildren with involved fathers have higher levels of self-control, self-esteem and social skills (Amato and Rivera, 1999). A **longitudinal** (30–year) study of teen mothers and their children (Foley and Furstenberg, 1999) provides strong evidence that fathers have a significant impact on the physical and mental health of their children. The study found two pathways through which father relationships in adolescence may benefit their children in adulthood. Both male and female children who felt close to a father in adolescence were significantly more likely to report better physical and mental health outcomes at age 27 net of their physical and mental health when they were teenagers (Foley and Furstenberg, 1999). Another longitudinal study (Sarkadi et al, 2008) shows that father engagement reduces the frequency of behavioural problems in boys and psychological problems in young women; it also enhances cognitive development while decreasing criminality and economic disadvantage in low-income families. The influence of a father's involvement on academic achievement extends into adolescence and young adulthood. When fathers are more involved in their child's school, children are more likely to do well academically (Pruett, 2000; Lamb, 2004; Rosenberg and Bradford, 2006).

However, involving fathers in their children's literacy activities may help fathers as well as their children. There are also numerous benefits that have been reported for the fathers themselves, including greater skill acquisition, greater confidence and self-esteem, a better father–child relationship, and increased engagement with learning (Clark, 2009).

From the woman's point of view, the stay-at-home dad arrangement allows the mother to work without having to use day care or a nanny. This arrangement saves mothers from having to deal with the stress of finding acceptable childcare, checking backgrounds and paying for care. This allows for a more relaxed working environment for the mother and allows her to focus on her career. If the mother has a higher-paying job, this extra income can go to savings for the benefit of the children. In their sample of male homemakers and female providers, Robertson and Verscheldon (1993) found that the female providers were most happy about the decision to have their male partners stay at home because it allowed them to have a fulfilling career without worrying about their children. Robertson and Verscheldon (1993) also found that both the male homemakers and female providers in their sample were more satisfied with their lives when compared to more traditional couples. It seems that if the partners of stay-at-home fathers are satisfied with the decision, then the fathers themselves are more likely to be happy being at home.

The househusbands'/stay-at-home fathers' movement

Society is still coming to terms with the concept of a stay-at-home father. Many women and men still find the lifestyle difficult to accept. Studies examining attitudes towards parents show that stay-at-home fathers were perceived more negatively than fathers who had the traditional breadwinning role ((Brescoll and Uhlmann, 2005; Petroski and Edley, 2006; Rochlen et al, 2007, 2010). Men – as well as women – who have been stay-at-home parents may also face prejudice when they attempt to enter or return to the workplace. Some companies are prejudiced against stay-at-home fathers, and many men simply 'take vacation leave' instead of family leave when a new baby comes. They know that it will affect their career and limit their path to promotions. Employers may also have inhibitions about hiring a person who has a six- to eight-year gap in his or her career. All in all, then, finding a job after the stay-at-home period may not be easy.

Thus, while more and more men are eager to spend more time at home, the stigma remains. In order to fight prejudice and also to create a means for the exchange of ideas, feelings and experiences, some stay-at-home husbands and fathers have taken the initiative of creating

Internet resources on their own. There are now several blogs and online forums where (American, Australian, Canadian, European, Japanese, etc) stay-at-home husbands and fathers get together and share their insights and reflections on their experiences. Among the websites are:

- Stay at Home Dads (see: http://www.stayathomedads.co.uk/): this website provides pieces of advice and information for all stay-at-home fathers everywhere. The site offers a news section, articles written by stay-at-home dads, information on money matters (advice on benefits, children's savings accounts and tax-free savings, insurance quotes, etc), a health section and some stay-at-home dads' views.
- Daddyshome – The National At-Home Dad Network (see: http://www.athomedad.org/): this is a non-profit corporation that is a community for stay-at-home dads, fathers who are the primary carer in their family and other involved dads.

A group of participants in these virtual communities have organised the 'At-Home Dads Convention',[11] which has been celebrated annually since 1995. The goal of this event is to bring together men who have crossed gender role boundaries. The convention features seminars and forums that provide further training and information on home management, family life and child-rearing. As embodied in their battle cry, 'Men who change diapers change the world', the convention also aims to help men to take on more responsibilities and become a more significant presence in their households, in childcare and in the lives of their children. We close this chapter by describing some features of the Italian stay-at-home men's movement (Ruspini, 2009, 2011b). Italy is an interesting case: on average, based on comparative international data, Italian men do less unpaid household work than do men in most other Organisation for Economic Co-operation and Development (OECD) countries, being second only to Japanese men. The Harmonized European Time Use Survey (HETUS)[12] found that Italian men perform the smallest amount of unpaid domestic work among men in the countries considered, while Italian women stand out as the least active in the labour market (Mencarini and Tanturri, 2004; Romano and Bruzzese, 2007; Bloemen, Pasqua, and Stancanelli, 2008; Tanturri and Mencarini, 2009).

The Italian Association of Househusbands (ASUC)[13] operates in this context. ASUC, a Tuscany-based association, is the first male organisation to enter the Fédération Européenne des Femmes Actives en Famille/European Federation of Parents and Carers at Home (FEFAF), which represents European at-home parents and carers at the

European Union level. ASUC is becoming more than just a gathering point for stay-at-home men. One of the main aims of the association is to support and to protect them. The ASUC website contains much practical information in order to help househusbands face domestic life on a daily basis. Examples include advice on: how to hang and dry clothes; how to do the laundry; how to sew a button; and how to deal with hard-to-remove stains. ASUC is now campaigning for men to be allowed to write 'househusband' on national ID cards. In Italy, many regional laws still do not permit this and so men are forced to write 'unemployed', even if they have chosen to stay at home. Fiorenzo Bresciani, President of ASUC, writes:

> Cooking, cleaning the house, the ability to take care of all those details which seem insignificant but make the art of home-dwelling an art have enthralled me more and more and made me reflect on how much gender prejudices and a culture rigidly linked to the stereotypes of a macho, virile male, had penalised us men, depriving us of the ability to take care of the persons living with us and the chance to enjoy the pleasures of home.[14]

Notes

[1] See the Glossary at the end of the book for a presentation of the key concepts used in this chapter (highlighted in bold on first mention).

[2] See: http://www.census.gov/population/socdemo/hh-fam/shp1.pdf (all websites cited in this chapter have been consulted in the period September–December 2012).

[3] See: http://en.wikipedia.org/wiki/Stay-at-home_dad

[4] See: http://sc2220.wetpaint.com/page/On+the+rise%3A+Stay-at-home+Dads

[5] Data for this article are drawn from several Australian Bureau of Statistics (ABS) surveys: the 1992 Family Survey, the 1997 and 2003 Family Characteristics Surveys, the monthly Labour Force Survey, the 2003 Persons Not in the Labour Force Survey, the 2003 Working Arrangements Survey and the 2002 Child Care Survey.

[6] The LFS provides estimates of employment and unemployment, which are among the most timely and important measures of performance of the

Canadian economy. With the release of the survey results only 13 days after the completion of data collection, the LFS estimates are the first of the major monthly economic data series to be released. The Canadian LFS was developed following the Second World War to satisfy a need for reliable and timely data on the labour market. Information was urgently required on the massive labour market changes involved in the transition from a war- to a peacetime economy. The main objective of the LFS is to divide the working-age population into three mutually exclusive classifications – employed, unemployed and not in the labour force – and to provide descriptive and explanatory data on each of these (see: http://www23.statcan.gc.ca/imdb/p2SV.pl?Function=getSurvey&SDDS=3701&lang=en&db=imdb&adm=8&dis=2).

[7] The study used grounded theory to explore the lives, decision-making processes and support systems of 14 full-time stay-at-home fathers. Recruitment methods included parenting listservs, local parenting websites, grocery stores and local playgroups. Interviews lasted between 60 and 90 minutes with the majority taking place in the participants' homes. The final sample included 13 married men and one man living with his female partner. Grounded theory methods are systematic methodologies involving the discovery of theory through the analysis of data. They are referred to as inductive in that they are a process of building theory up from the data itself (Glaser and Strauss, 1967).

[8] The Canadian study that informs this research is a qualitative study of over 100 fathers who self-identified as primary carers; included here were 70 stay-at-home fathers (66 fathers who were at home for at least one year, and four fathers who were on parental leave). The Belgian research was focused on a sample of 21 fathers who lived with a professionally active partner, and who had stayed at home for at least six months with the explicit aim of taking care of their children.

[9] Interviews with 70 stay-at-home fathers were conducted between 2000 and 2003 in the following ways: 48 in person (46 face-to-face interviews and two fathers through focus groups), 12 by telephone and 10 by Web correspondence. Web correspondence was used in order to attract a larger number of fathers to the study as well as to include fathers who might prefer a more limited involvement in the project. In the end, one third of the Web-based surveys with stay-at-home fathers (ie 5/15) were followed up with face-to-face or telephone interviews. The Web-based data were viewed as a supplement to the main data set of in-depth interviews.

[10] The sample for the study were 118 Canadian fathers who self-defined as primary carers of their children (mainly single fathers and stay-at-home fathers). Of the 118 fathers who participated in the study, nearly two thirds of the fathers (62) were interviewed through in-depth face-to-face individual interviews, 27 through telephone interviews, 12 in three focus groups and 17 through internet correspondence. Moreover, 28 fathers were interviewed two to three times using different methods.

[11] See: http://www.athomedadconvention.com

[12] Since the early 1990s, Eurostat – the statistical office of the European Union situated in Luxembourg and tasked with providing the European Union with statistics at the European level that enable comparisons between countries and regions – has supported a series of projects aiming at harmonising time use statistics in the European Union. As a result of the efforts carried out by Eurostat in collaboration with a number of national statistical institutes, Eurostat developed recommendations (guidelines) for harmonised European time use surveys in order to ensure that member states were in the position to implement time use surveys on a comparable European basis. The guidelines were developed during the late 1990s and a final draft was published in 2000. Most national statistical institutes around Europe that have carried out time use surveys since the late 1990s have taken the guidelines into account. The HETUS database currently contains 15 European countries (see: https://www.h2.scb.se/tus/tus/).

[13] See: http://www.uominicasalinghi.it/index.asp?pg=1321

[14] See: http://www.uominicasalinghi.it

References

ABS (Australian Bureau of Statistics) (2006) 'Fathers' work and family balance', 4102.0 Australian Social Trends. Available at: http://www.abs.gov.au/ausstats/abs@.nsf/bb8db737e2af84b8ca2571780015701e/acf29854f8c8509eca2571b00010329b!OpenDocument

Allen, S.M. and Daly, K. (2002) 'The effects of father involvement: a summary of the research evidence', *The FII-ONews*, 1, pp 1–11.

Amato, P.R. and Rivera, F. (1999) 'Father–child relations, mother–child relations, and offspring psychological well-being in early adulthood', *Journal of Marriage and Family*, vol 56, no 4, pp 1031-42.

Bloemen, H.G., Pasqua, S. and Stancanelli, E.G.F. (2008) 'An empirical analysis of the time allocation of Italian couples: are Italian men irresponsive?', IZA Discussion Paper No 3823, November.

Brescoll, V.L. and Uhlmann, E.L. (2005) 'Attitudes towards traditional and nontraditional parents', *Psychology of Women Quarterly*, vol 29, pp 436–45.

Burgess, A. (2005) 'Fathers and public services', in K. Stanley (ed) *Daddy dearest: active fatherhood and public policy*, London: Institute for Public Policy Research, pp 57-74.

Clark, C. (2009) 'Why fathers matter to their children's literacy', National Literacy Trust, June. Available at: http://www.literacytrust.org.uk/assets/0000/0770/Father_review_2009.pdf

Coltrane, S. (1996) *Family man: fatherhood, housework, and gender equity*, Oxford: Oxford University Press.

Coltrane, S. and Ishii–Kuntz, M. (1992) 'Men's housework: a life course perspective', *Journal of Marriage and the Family*, vol 54, pp 43–57.

Connell, R.W. (1987) *Gender and power*, Cambridge: Polity Press.

Connell, R.W. (1995) *Masculinities*, Cambridge: Polity Press; Sydney: Allen & Unwin; Berkeley: University of California Press. Second edition, 2005.

Connell, R.W. (2000) *The men and the boys*, Berkeley, CA: University of California Press.

Doucet, A. (2004) '"It's almost like I have a job, but I don't get paid": fathers at home reconfiguring work, care, and masculinity', *Fathering*, vol 2, no 3, pp 277–303. Available at: http://www.andreadoucet.com/wp-content/uploads/2011/02/Doucet-2005-Its-Almost-Like-I-Have-a-Job.pdf

Doucet, A. (2006) *Do men mother? Fathering, care, and domestic responsibility*, Toronto: University of Toronto Press.

Doucet, A. and Merla, L. (2007) 'Stay-at-home fathering. A strategy for balancing work and home in Canadian and Belgian families', *Community, Work and Family*, vol 10, no 4, pp 455–73. Available at: http://www.andreadoucet.com/wp-content/uploads/2010/11/Doucet-Merla-2007-Stay-at-Home-Fathering.pdf

Edwards, T. (2006) *Cultures of masculinity*, London and New York, NY: Routledge.

Fischer, J. and Anderson, V.N. (2012) 'Gender role attitudes and characteristics of stay-at-home and employed fathers', *Psychology of Men and Masculinity*, vol 13, no 1, pp 16–31.

Foley, K.A. and Furstenberg, F.F. (1999) *Paternal involvement and children's health: A Longitudinal Study*, Paper presented at the first biannual conference of the Urban Seminar Series on Children's Health and Safety on Fatherhood, Cambridge, Massachusetts. Available at: http://www.hks.harvard.edu/urbanpoverty/Urban%20Seminars/May1999/furstenberg.pdf

Giles, J. (2004) *The parlour and the suburb: domestic identities, class, femininity and modernity*, Oxford: Berg.

Glaser, B.G and Strauss, A. (1967) *Discovery of grounded theory. Strategies for qualitative research*, Chicago, IL: Aldine.

Greenstein, T.N. (1996) 'Husbands' participation in domestic labor: interactive effects of wives' and husbands' gender ideologies', *Journal of Marriage and the Family*, vol 58, pp 585–95.

Hoffman, J. (2008) 'Canadian dads @home'. Available at: http://www.fira.ca/article.php?id=140

Iacuone, D. (2005) '"Real men are tough guys": hegemonic masculinity and safety in the construction industry', *The Journal of Men's Studies*, vol 13, no 2, pp 247–66.

Kimmel, M.S. (1995) *The politics of manhood*, Philadelphia, PA: Temple University Press.

Kimmel, M.S. (1996) *Manhood in America. A cultural history*, New York, NY: Free Press.

Lamb, M.E. (ed) (2004) *The role of the father in child development* (4th edn), Hoboken, NJ: John Wiley & Sons.

Marsiglio, W. and Roy, K. (2012) *Nurturing dads. Social initiatives for contemporary fatherhood*, New York, NY: Russel Sage Foundation.

Mencarini, L. and Tanturri, M.L. (2004) 'Time use, family role-set and childbearing among Italian working women', *Genus*, vol LX, no 1, pp 111–37.

Petroski, D.J. and Edley, P.P. (2006) 'Stay-at-home fathers: masculinity, family, work and gender stereotypes', *The Electronic Journal of Communication*, vol 16, nos 3/4. Available at: http://www.cios.org/EJCPUBLIC/016/3/01634.HTML

Pruett, K.D. (2000) *Fatherneed: why father care is as essential as mother care for your child*, New York, NY: The Free Press.

Robertson, J.M. and Verschelden, C. (1993) 'Voluntary male homemakers and female providers: reported experiences and perceived social reactions', *The Journal of Men's Studies*, vol 1, no 4, pp 383-402.

Rochlen, A.B., McKelley, R.A., Suizzo, M.P. and Scaringi, V. (2007) 'Predictors of relationship satisfaction, psychological well-being, and life satisfaction among stay-at-home fathers', *Psychology of Men and Masculinity*, vol 11, no 4, pp 7–14.

Rochlen, A.B., McKelley, R.A., Suizzo, M.P. and Scaringi, V. (2008) '"I'm just providing for my family": a qualitative study of stay-at-home fathers', *Psychology of Men and Masculinity*, vol 8, no 4, pp 193–206. Available at: http://www.apa.org/pubs/journals/features/men-9-4-193.pdf

Rochlen, A.B., McKelley, R.A. and Whittaker, T.A. (2010) 'Stay-at-home fathers' reasons for entering the role and stigma experiences: a preliminary report', *Psychology of Men and Masculinity*, vol 11, no 4, pp 279–85.

Rohner, R.P. and Veneziano, R.A. (2001) 'The importance of father love: history and contemporary evidence', *Review of General Psychology*, vol 5, no 4, pp 382–405.

Romano, M.C. and Bruzzese, D. (2007) 'Fathers' participation in the domestic activities of everyday life', *Social Indicators Research*, vol 84, no 1, pp 97–116. Available at: http://www.springerlink.com/content/8224738341556637/fulltext.html

Rosenberg, J. and Bradford, W.W. (2006) 'The importance of fathers in the healthy development of children', Office on Child Abuse and Neglect, US Children's Bureau. Available at: http://www.childwelfare.gov/pubs/usermanuals/fatherhood/chaptertwo.cfm

Ruspini, E. (2009) 'Italian forms of masculinity between familism and social change', *Culture, Society & Masculinities*, vol 1, no 2, pp 121–36. Available at: http://www.highbeam.com/doc/1P3-1923637731.html

Ruspini, E. (2011a) 'L'uomo casalingo è un ossimoro?' ['Is the househusband an oxymoron?'], in M.L. Fagiani and E. Ruspini (eds) *Maschi alfa, beta, omega. Virilità italiane tra persistenze, imprevisti e mutamento*, Milano: FrancoAngeli, pp 95–112.

Ruspini, E. (2011b) 'And yet something is on the move: education for new forms of masculinity and paternity in Italy', in E. Ruspini, J. Hearn, B. Pease and K. Pringle (eds) *Men and masculinities around the world. Transforming men's practices*, Basingstoke: Palgrave Macmillan, pp 59–69.

Sarkadi, A., Kristiansson, R., Oberklaid, F. and Bremberg, S. (2008) 'Fathers' involvement and children's developmental outcomes: a systematic review of longitudinal studies', *Acta Pediatrica*, vol 97, pp 153–8.

Snarey, J. and Vaillant, G.E. (2002) *How fathers care for the next generation: a four-decade study*, Cambridge, MA: Harvard University Press.

Sussman, D. and Bonnell, S. (2006) 'Wives as primary breadwinners', *Perspectives on Labour and Income*, vol 7, no 8, pp 52-97. Available at: http://www.statcan.gc.ca/pub/75-001-x/10806/9291-eng.htm

Tanturri, M.L. and Mencarini, L. (2009) 'Fathers' involvement in daily childcare activities in Italy: does a work–family reconciliation issue exist?', ChilD Working Paper no 22/2009. Available at: http://annazavaritt.blog.ilsole24ore.com/files/fathers-involvement-in-daily-childcare-activities.pdf

US Department of Health and Human Services (2004) 'Building blocks for father involvement', Administration on Children, Youth and Families. Available at: http://www.headstartresourcecenter.org/fatherhood/Resources/root/data/Building%20Blocks/HSBCombo4.1.pdf

Winkler, A.E. (1998) 'Earnings of husbands and wives in dual-earner families', *Monthly Labor Review*, vol 121, no 4, pp 42–8.

CHAPTER FIVE

Lone mothers and lone fathers

Lone mothers and lone fathers through history

The chapter will reflect upon forms and characteristics of lone parenting (also lone parenthood) in Western nations. A lone-parent family usually comprises an adult (a woman or a man) living without a partner and with one or more (dependent) children. The parent not living with a spouse or partner has most of the day-to-day responsibilities in raising the child or children. As we will see later on, the last three decades of the 20th century saw a marked increase in the number of lone mothers and fathers and in the interest in this population by social science researchers. Today, lone parents are one of the most challenging family forms (see, eg, Klett-Davies, 2007). In many countries, social workers are increasingly faced with meeting the complex needs of these mothers, fathers and their children.

The term 'lone' parent has come into more common use in recent years. As Caballero and Edwards (2010, pp 3–4) write:

> 'Lone mother families' is a relatively modern umbrella term for mothers with dependent children but without fathers, as a consequence variously of never being partnered, being separated or divorced, or the death of a partner. During the 1960s, for example, the term was virtually unknown.... At the time, most lone mothers were widowed, but over the latter part of the 1960s divorce began to eclipse death as the primary route into lone motherhood.

Lone parents are certainly not a new phenomenon (Lewis, 1997; Bimbi, 2000; Simoni, 2000; Terragni, 2000; Larkin, 2009). In history, there are different examples of families with children and without one of the two parents, for example: spouses who died prematurely; fathers who moved away from their families; and women who became pregnant without being married (Skevik, 2001). For a long time, unmarried mothers have dominated welfare discourses: they have featured in policies for nearly two centuries. The stigmatisation of single motherhood also pervades the history of welfare discourse: single-parent families traditionally have been deemed a part of the 'underclass' – that is, the segment of the population that occupies the lowest possible position in a class hierarchy, usually composed of the disadvantaged – as compared to the nuclear, traditional family (Marsden, 1969). The origins of this stigma lie deep in history. Following Swain and Howe (1995), it had both a moral and an economic base: an attempt to safeguard the institution of marriage while minimising the cost of transgressions for those who have an obligation to maintain the poor.

We will now give some examples. Throughout English history, there has been a stigma attached to being an illegitimate child and these children have suffered from discrimination and prejudice through no fault of their own (Beatson et al, 2011). The English Poor Law 1834 addressed the concerns about increasing illegitimacy and the related increased demand for poor relief. The Poor Law Commissioners' Report of 1834 influenced the Poor Law 1834. The Commissioners thought that poor men were at the mercy of blackmail and perjury by women with illegitimate children. Under the 1834 Act, illegitimate children were the responsibility of their mothers until they were 16 years old. If mothers were unable to support themselves and their children, they usually entered the workhouse, whereas the father was free of responsibility for his illegitimate children. Not surprisingly, the 1834 Act did not reduce illegitimacy. It increased because it enabled men to avoid some of the responsibility for their illegitimate children (Beatson et al, 2011). Fortunately, this 1834 law on illegitimate children was unpopular and was replaced with a subsequent Act in 1844 (7&8 Vict. c. 101), allowing an unmarried mother to order the father to pay for maintenance of the mother and child, whether or not she was receiving poor relief (Glicken, 2013, p 25). The same is true for Italian fascist policy.[1] Following Bimbi's (1997) arguments, lone mothers were stigmatised in fascist social policy, which was directed towards safeguarding the health and morals of the younger generations. Unmarried mothers were negatively portrayed as being 'immoral' and seen to be less deserving than other people who were poor (De Grazia, 1992; Kerzer, 1993; Lewis, 1997; Bimbi, 1997). In Australia, until the early 1970s, women were assumed to have husbands who were breadwinners and expected to be housewives and to raise children themselves (Swain and Howe, 1995). Historically, there has been a stigma attached to sole mothering in particular, with single mothers being seen as immoral, to blame for their unmarried state and less desirable community members (Stanley et al, 2005). In a final example, following Huda (2001), the Personal Responsibility and Work Opportunity Reconciliation Act (PRWORA), enacted in August 1996 by President Clinton, stigmatises dependence and ascribes moral fault to one particular group: poor single mothers. PRWORA imposes strict time limits and stringent work requirements in the name of 'family values' and 'independence'. PRWORA's 'pro-family' and 'pro-work' rhetoric and provisions privilege marital status and implicitly and explicitly condemn child-rearing and childbearing outside of marriage. The moral tenor of PRWORA reflects an entrenched cultural perception of single motherhood as pathological (Huda, 2001).

Research on lone parenting

Researching lone parenting is not an easy task. One major problem complicates research on lone mothers and fathers, especially in a comparative perspective: the lack of a standard definition of lone-parent households and its implications for empirical social research. This exerts an impact on the availability of comparable data sets for the study of lone-parent families. This is due to the fact that lone parenting is a multifaceted and dynamic experience. Lone parenthood is a status that people come into in a variety of ways: divorce, long-lasting separations, desertion, death of a partner, birth of a child outside marriage or child abuse/neglect. (In case of neglect/maltreatment, children may been removed/taken away from the unfit parent. An unfit parent is a person, mother or father, who neglects his or her child in such a way that puts the child at risk, such as failing to take them to school regularly, failing to provide basic necessities, putting them in danger physically or mentally on a regular basis, and so on. If a parent is found to be unfit, the child may be put in the custody of the other parent. The other parent then becomes a 'lone' mother or father.) There are also different routes out: marriage, remarriage, cohabitation, placing children for adoption and children growing up and leaving home.

There are, indeed, many issues involved in settling on a specific definition of lone-parent households. In particular, we need to determine the age limit for the children, the marital status of the head, whether to include cohabitants as single and whether to include single parents who are co-residing with other relatives, such as the grandparents of the children (see, eg, González, 2008). One research report on the situation of lone parents in Italy, Germany, Poland, France and the UK (EU Lifelong Learning Program Leonardo da Vinci Transfer of Innovation[2]) shows significant differences in the definition of lone parenting between these countries: some countries recognise the break-up of a cohabiting relationship as equivalent to the divorce of married persons, and some do not. For example, the Italian National Institute of Statistics (*Istituto*

Nazionale di Statistica; ISTAT) defines a lone-parent family as a family composed of only one adult (widowed, divorced, single). In Germany, the definition of lone parents used by the Federal Ministry for Family, Senior Citizens, Women and Youth is the following: mothers or fathers who are unmarried, widowed, separated or divorced, who live with their child or children up to the age of 18 years in one household. In Poland, a lone-parent household refers to a household in which a single adult lives alone with one or several children. According to the French National Institute for Statistics and Research (*Institut National de la Statistique et des Etudes Economiques*; INSEE), a lone parent is a parent with full-time responsibility for the care of one or more single children under the age of 25 (with the condition that none of these children have children). For the UK General Household Survey,[3] a lone-parent family consists of one parent, irrespective of sex, living with his or her never-married dependent children, provided these children have no children of their own. The UK Census further specifies that the children only count as dependent if they are aged either under 16 or from 16 to (under) 19 and undertaking full-time education. Gingerbread Northern Ireland[4] – the lead agency working with and for one-parent families in Northern Ireland – expands the term 'lone parent' to include parents who have full custody of children while the spouse/partner is in long-term institutional care (ie prison or long-term hospitalisation). Gingerbread Northern Ireland also expands the definition of a dependent child to include: any child under the age of 18 years; a person who is over 18 years and due to a physical or mental disability is unable to become independent of his/her parent; or a person pursuing education/training who is unable to become independent of his/her parent. In a final example, for the International Encyclopedia of Marriage and Family,[5] a lone-parent family is a family where a parent lives with dependent children, either alone or in a larger household, without a spouse or partner.

Notwithstanding these methodological challenges and problems, existing research has underlined some interesting trends:

1. One-parent families are growing in number, although at different rates and with different features, in all the countries of the Western world.
2. The characteristics of lone mothers and fathers are not homogeneous between local cultures and contexts. Moreover, the lone-parent population is not static: people move in and out of this condition. The one-parent condition is now viewed as a 'stage' in family life:

lone parenting may only be a temporary, transitional stage in the family formation process (see, eg, Cliquet, 2003).
3. Lone parenthood is a universally gendered phenomenon. The lone parent is mainly a woman. However, the number of lone fathers is growing.
4. A further, important common factor in international statistics is that one-parent families/households constitute a disadvantaged group in terms of financial, personal and time resources.

Each of these issues will now be discussed in detail.

The number of lone parents is growing

The fastest-growing group of lone parents is now single or never-married lone mothers. In the US,[6] there was a dramatic increase in single-parent families in the last three decades of the 20th century; whereas only 13% of families were headed by a single parent in 1970. Following Feltey (2003), approximately 84% of these families are headed by women. Of all single-parent families, the most common are those headed by divorced or separated mothers (58%), followed by never-married mothers (24%). Other family heads include widows (7%), divorced and separated fathers (8.4%), never-married fathers (1.5%), and widowers (0.9%). There is ethnic variation in the proportion of families headed by a single parent: 22% for white, 57% for black and 33% for Hispanic families.[7] In France, the number of one-parent families has been rising steadily since 1980. They totalled less than 900,000 in 1982 (10% of families), and almost 1.8 million (20%) in 2005. In three quarters of cases, the parents are separated, in 15% of cases, the family is founded by a single mother and in 10%, the second parent has died and the surviving parent has not formed a new couple.[8] In Germany, the number of lone mothers has almost tripled since the early 1970s: never-married mothers are now the most common type of lone mothers with dependent children (Klett-Davies, 2007). In the UK, there were around 2 million lone parents with dependent children in 2011. Office for National Statistics (ONS) figures show that the number of lone-parent families with dependent children in the UK went up from 1,745,000 in 2001 to 1,958,000 in 2011.[9] Over the same period, the number of married couples dropped from 12.3 million to 12 million. The ONS found that 92% of lone parents are mothers and that women are more likely to take the main responsibilities for any children when relationships break down. The same figures show that more than one in four families (26%) are now led by a single parent.

In Ireland, between 1996 and 2002, the number of one-parent families increased by 25%. There was also a rise of almost 50% in the number of lone parents with children under 15 who live in poverty between 1994 and 2004 (Combat Poverty Agency, 2006). The Australian Bureau of Statistics (ABS, 2006) shows that, in Australia, in 2004–06, there were on average 486,000 one-parent families with children under 15 years.[10] They accounted for 22% of all families with children of this age. In this period, on average, one in five children aged under 15 years (20%) were in one-parent families. Over the last two decades, one-parent families increased substantially as a proportion of all Australian families with children under 15 years. In 1986–88, one-parent families accounted for 14% of such families on average. The proportion increased to an average of 20% in 1996–98, reached 23% in 2002–04 and then fell slightly to 22% in 2004–06.[11]

This growth is linked to different elements. Developed countries, in particular, are experiencing an increase in single-parent families as separation and divorce become more common. Historically, lone-parent families were the result of parental death; in the US about one quarter of children born around the turn of the 19th century experienced the death of a parent before they reached age 15 (Amato, 2000a; see also the *Encyclopedia of Marriage and Family*[12]). The factors most commonly related to the contemporary one-parent family are changing social and cultural trends, increased rates of divorce and non-marital childbearing, increased employment opportunities for women, decreased employment opportunities for men, and the availability of welfare benefits that enable women to set up their own households (Rodgers, 1996). Lone-parent households are also increasing because of the growing number of mothers and fathers who are 'single' by choice (Miller, 1992; Hertz, 2006): men and women who have deliberately chosen to have children outside a permanent relationship. Unmarried women beyond the teen years may become mothers via several routes: national or international adoption, pregnancy with male partners or insemination by (known or unknown) donors. In her book on unmarried mothers, Rosanna Hertz (2006) interviewed 65 women – ranging from physicians and financial analysts to social workers, teachers and secretaries. These women decided to have a child through medically assisted procreation or adoption. In Hertz's vision, these women resist the myth of an 'appropriate family life' and construct a family life for themselves and their children outside the boundaries of normative, heterosexual families.

The experience of lone parenting may be very different

Researchers examining lone parents have repeatedly noted the wide range of cultural and material circumstances and the variety of personal experiences and feelings involved (see, eg, Haddon and Silverstone, 1994; Rowlingson and McKay, 1998, 2005; Cliquet, 2003; Caballero and Edwards, 2010; Ruspini, 2010; Mata, 2011). Some are lone parents as a result of marital instability (lone mothers and fathers who are divorced and separated); others are single, widows and widowers. On the question of gender, lone fathers are more likely to be widowers with older children and, hence, have a slightly different experience of lone parenting from that of the majority of lone mothers (Rowlingson, 2001). Data on ethnicity points to the variation of lone parenthood among different ethnic groups. There are also geographical variations, with a considerable concentration of lone parents in inner cities (Haddon and Silverstone, 1994). And we should not forget about lesbian, gay, bisexual, **transsexual**, **transgender**, intersex and **queer** (LGBTTIQ) one-parent families (see, eg, Ruspini, 2010). A further, final consideration is that, at least in some countries, many unmarried mothers are living together with a partner (who may or may not be the father of the child[ren]). Others may live in multigenerational households, for example, in co-residence with their families of origin (DeLeire and Kalil, 2001). In Japan, as Tokoro (2003) writes, the number of lone parents varies, depending on surveys, partly due to the fact that a number of lone parents live with their elderly parents and they are often treated as three-generation households. Many lone mothers and fathers, in other words, are not necessarily *lone* parents.

As lone parenting is a complex and dynamic experience, the incidence of one-parent families varies a great deal across European countries. A longitudinal study (González, 2008), which has explored the sources of the cross-country variation in the incidence of single-mother families in Europe over the period 1994–2001, using data from the European Community Household Panel (ECHP),[13] shows that there is significant variation in the prevalence of lone mothers across countries. This can be attributed to differences in mainly three demographic rates: non-marital fertility, divorce and co-residence (with relatives other than a partner). The low number of lone mothers in Spain, Portugal, Italy and Greece can be attributed to very low levels of non-marital fertility (less than 5% of never-married women reported having children in 2001), very low divorce rates (less than 6% of ever-married women were divorced) and high co-residence (more than 50% of never-married mothers were not living by themselves with their children). The most extreme case is probably Greece, where just 5% of never-married women had children in 2001 and essentially all of them were in co-residence, while only 5% of ever-married women were divorced, and more than half of all divorced mothers were in co-residence. At the other end of the spectrum, the high prevalence of lone mothers in Sweden is the result of high non-marital fertility (25% of never-married women have children), very low co-residence (just 1% of never-married mothers) and high divorce rates (14% of ever-married women). The UK has higher co-residence, but very high divorce rates (19% of ever-married women in 2001). The number of lone mothers doubled in The Netherlands between 1994 and 2001. This change can mainly be attributed to large increases in divorce rates and non-marital fertility. A further consideration is that, as said above, the lone-parent family is now viewed as a 'stage' in family life that lasts on average about five-and-a-half years. Lone motherhood (and fatherhood) may be only a temporary, transitional stage in the process of family formation (Cliquet, 2003). Following Cliquet (2003), many unmarried mothers are not necessarily to be considered as lone parents. Single motherhood by 'choice', more particularly among older, better-educated, working women, also seems to be on the rise (Miller, 1992).

Lone-parent families are mostly headed by women

This can be explained if we think that mothers' greater responsibility in childcare is culturally and institutionally confirmed in legal practice when deciding on the custody of children in divorce or separation proceedings. In the great majority of cases of both divorce and separation, under-age children are entrusted to their mother. According to the ONS, in 2006, nine out of 10 lone-parent families in Great Britain were headed by a woman (ONS, 2007). In 2011, women accounted for 92% of lone parents with dependent children and men accounted for 8% of lone parents with dependent children. These percentages have changed little since 2001.[14] In France, in 2005, out of 16 million children aged under 25 still living in their parents' home, 2.8 million, that is, more than one in six, lived in a single-parent family. Their proportion increases with age: 10% of children under two live with a single parent, and 24% at ages 17–24. Children most often live with their mother (in 86% of cases). However, lone fathers are also growing in number. For example, from 1995 to 2006, the proportion of Canadian fathers who were lone parents rose from 5% to 8%. The number of lone-parent fathers stood at more than 338,000 in 2006 (Beaupré et al, 2010). The Australian Bureau of Statistics shows that, in

2006, 87% of one-parent families with children under 15 years were headed by mothers. The proportion headed by fathers was 12% in 1997 and 13% in 2006 (see also Greif, 1992).[15]

Lone parents (and especially lone mothers) are more likely than any other social group to be living in poverty

Previous research (see for example Roll, 1992; Duncan and Edwards, 1997; Edin and Lein, 1997; Lewis, 1997; National Council for One Parent Families, 1999; Bimbi, 2000; Pedersen et al, 2000; Bradbury et al, 2001; Millar and Ridge, 2001; Millar and Rowlingson, 2001; Ruspini, 2001; Rowlingson and McKay, 2005) has established that lone mothers have, on average, particularly low levels of income, exposing themselves and their children to various forms of hardship. In the international, comparative perspective, single parents may be viewed as a highly disadvantaged group in terms of their resources, which include money, time and social networks. But it has been difficult to identify cause and effect because of lack of data tracking lone-parent families and their circumstances over time. Data from the EU Survey on Income and Living Conditions (EU-SILC)[16] shows that in 2009, 16.6% of lone parents were living in consistent poverty, as compared to 5.5% of the population as a whole.[17] Lone mothers also have poorer health overall than couple mothers (Millar and Ridge, 2001). Their worse state of health emerges from individual reports and from a greater use of health services (see, eg, Popay and Jones, 1990; Benzeval, 1998; Baker and North, 1999). They are more liable to suffer from depression and physical and psychological disturbances (see, among others, Brown and Moran, 1997), closely linked to heavy workloads in the family, lack of time and precarious economic conditions. Lone mothers, especially if adolescent, are also more exposed to pathologies during pregnancy and health complications during delivery, and their children to poor conditions of health in the years following birth (Fraser et al, 1995; Cunnington, 2001; Berthoud and Robson, 2001).

However, being a lone mother (or father) does not in itself constitute a necessary and sufficient condition to determine a situation of need. There is no causal relationship or inevitable association between lone parenthood and poverty. In the case of women, their disproportionate vulnerability to poverty is the result of complex but mutually reinforcing threads, whose origins lie in the limitations placed upon women by the current gendered division of labour and by the (inherent) assumption that women are dependent on men (Sands and Nuccio, 1989; Scheiwe, 1994). The economic difficulties faced are aggravated by other factors, such as: lack of childcare facilities, which play a crucial role in facilitating women's full-time employment; concentration of women in lower-status and lower-paid jobs, since their participation in paid employment needs to accommodate their domestic commitments; inflexible working hours; inadequate vocational education and training programmes; and problems related to housing. Female heads of families with young dependent children have less opportunity of finding employment because of working conditions and the responsibility for child-rearing. Following Albelda, Himmelweit and Humphries (2005), lone parents face difficult decisions in allocating their time to caring and income generation, but there is only one adult in their families to do both; further, that one adult is mainly a woman, who will generally earn less than a man, compounding the difficulties. Lone parents must therefore rely on a range of support mechanisms (partners, other family members, friends, neighbours, employers and government policy) to manage; they can therefore rarely be socially and economically **independent** (please see the term **independence** in the glossary). As Hertz (2006) writes, single mothers 'orchestrate a network to substitute for a man' and this network provides various levels of support. Nevertheless, single mothers pay a high price for their constant negotiation. Lone mothers have to make sacrifices that often lead to not taking promotions and finding employment that is less demanding and, hence, less rewarding. The difficulties that lone mothers have to face within the labour market and domestic dimensions are multiplied if we think that the institutional framework is still not ready to give an answer to the needs of lone-parent families (see, eg, Hobson, 1994; Scheiwe, 1994; Swain and Howe, 1995; Lewis, 1997). Social policy in this area is inherently contradictory, encouraging lone mothers into paid employment on the one hand, while demanding greater involvement of mothers in their children's lives on the other.

The case of young lone mothers is particularly interesting (see, for example, Singh and Darroch, 2000; Cunnington, 2001; Daguerre and Nativel, 2008). Young lone mothers have often not completed their education and do not have permanent work (and, hence, have not achieved sufficient levels of professional or social capital) or a partner and, for emergency reasons, are forced to remain with (or return to) their family of origin. A reading of the British Household Panel Survey (BHPS),[18] regarding 500 women interviewed for the first time at the age of 18 and re-interviewed the following year, examined the dynamic relationship between adolescent pregnancies and educational chances (quoted in Berthoud and Robson, 2001). What emerged is that motherhood constitutes an event able to strongly interfere with learning processes and with investment in education. Two effects in particular emerged: first, young 18-year-old women with low educational levels proved to be more likely to start a pregnancy in the period between the first interview and the second than more educated women; and, second, compared with women without children, young women who were already mothers at the age of 18 showed little likelihood (less than 50%) of achieving additional educational qualifications between year t and year $t + 1$ (and, hence, to invest in education and training). In the case of young lone mothers, then, the presence of children may be considered as a negative index of social capital – seen as a system of relationship networks, bonds with family or relatives, and social membership, ascribed or acquired – in that it limits the possibility of cultivating relationships and, hence, to activate a synergy between the networks available, which, above all, take on a particular gender form.[19]

In terms of time, young lone mothers have considerably anticipated the reproductive function. In their lives, motherhood precedes the conclusion of their education, their entry into the labour market, their leaving their family and their stable cohabitation with a partner. This sequence of events appears 'anomalous' if we think that the transition process towards adulthood is today increasingly marked by delays: the lengthening of education; the search for a satisfactory, long-term job; the period preceding the setting up of a stable relationship; and the time gap between establishing a relationship and the decision to have children. Within a context of growing uncertainty, fragmentation, diversity and also risk, the 'ideal' transition to adulthood seems to be the outcome of a sequence of events that ends with the decision to leave home 'at the right time', after having completed education, started a high-quality and financially rewarding job, and finding a good partner and, possibly, legalised the union (Leccardi and Ruspini, 2006; Ruspini, 2006).

Lone parenting and children

Substantial research evidence shows that, on average, children who have experienced parental divorce score somewhat lower than children in first-marriage families on measures of social and emotional well-being, educational attainment, academic performance and physical health (Amato and Booth, 1997; Amato, 2000b). Children in divorced families are more likely to repeat a grade and to have higher drop-out rates and lower rates of college graduation. Due to a shortage of education, they do not have good opportunities to find a job. Some children decide to leave home when their parents separate. Especially in lone-mother families, children tend to experience: short- and long-term economic and psychological disadvantages; higher absentee rates at school, lower levels of education and higher drop-out rates (with boys more negatively affected than girls); and more delinquent activity, including alcohol and drug addiction. Adolescents, on the other hand, seems to be more negatively affected by parental discord prior to divorce than by living in single-parent families and actually gain in responsibility as a result of altered family routines (Demo and Acock, 1991; Acock and Demo, 1994). Children in single-mother homes are also more likely to experience health-related problems as a result of the decline in their living standard, including the lack of health insurance (Mauldin, 1990). Later, as children from one-parent families become adults, they are more likely to marry early, have children early and divorce. Girls are at greater risk of becoming single mothers as a result of non-marital childbearing or divorce (McLanahan and Booth, 1989). A common explanation for the problems found among the children of single parents has been the absence of a male adult in the family (Gongla, 1982). The relationship between children and non-custodial fathers can be difficult and strained but the absence of a father in the family can, as we have seen in Chapter Four, have implications beyond childhood (Pruett, 2000; Lamb, 2004; Rosenberg and Bradford, 2006; Flood, 2007). The economic deprivation of lone-parent families, in combination with other sources of strain and stress, is a major source of the problems experienced by both parents and children.

However, the majority of children adjust and recover and do not experience severe problems over time (Coontz, 1997). As Acock and Demo (1994) note, children and adolescents in divorced families vary widely in their adjustment; that is, many children exhibit aggressive behaviour, difficulties with peers and low self-esteem following their parents' divorce, while many others adjust readily and think highly of themselves. Children's adjustment within any particular family structure (eg first-marriage families, divorced families, reconstituted families) varies along a continuum from very poor adjustment to very positive adjustment, with many children and adolescents faring better post-divorce than their counterparts living in first-marriage families. Moreover, some of these problems may be attributed to a decrease in available resources and adult supervision; many of the negative effects disappear when there is adequate supervision, income and continuity in social networks (McLanahan and Sandefur, 1994).

However, lone parenting has also shown positive effects on children.[20] First of all, lone parents tend to create closer and stronger bonds with their children. Lone parenting involves looking after the child's requirements alone, which amounts to a lot of time spent with them.

Lone parents also tend to treat their children with more responsibility and maturity. The child becomes their confidant, pal and partner. This initiates a general level of maturity in the children and they turn out to be more understanding and responsible than their contemporaries.

Children reared by single parents have quite a different outlook towards life. They treat every moment as a teaching experience: this makes them more confident and independent. Lone parents, as said earlier, usually seek help, solidarity and assistance from their relatives, friends, colleagues or neighbours to raise their children. This introduces community life to the child at a relatively early age and empowers them with the ability to socialise and understand the human variety.

Therefore, there is an urgent need to introduce certain measures to highlight the positive effects of lone parenting, and ensure the all-round development of a child, instead of focusing only on the negative aspects of family life.

The lone parenthood movement: from marginalisation to empowerment

The relationship between lone parenting and information and communication technologies (ICTs) has not yet been fully explored (among the existing studies, see Haddon and Silverstone, 1994; Haddon, 2000). It would, however, be legitimate in principle to ask what role ICTs might play in relation to lone parents' social exclusion. As said in the introductory chapter to this book, advanced internet technologies and Web 2.0 may play a key role in mediating the public and the private in the lives of groups such as lone parents and may enhance their abilities to fulfil active roles in society. They may offer an alternative window on the world compared to existing broadcast media; they can also play an important role in facilitating the logistics of everyday life.

Starting from these premises, there are now several websites where lone mothers and fathers may get and keep in touch and share their insights and reflections on their experiences. Among the existing websites:

• One Parent Families Association of Canada (see: http://www.oneparentfamiliesassociation.ca/): its missions are: first, to develop and provide a broad comprehensive programme for the enlightenment and guidance of single parents and their children on the special needs they encounter; second, to develop and provide broad and comprehensive programmes of group activities and recreational activities for single parents and their children; third, to provide the children with a sense of shared experience; fourth, to encourage and develop the interchange among members of experience and knowledge relating to their special needs; fifth, to make the benefit of that experience available at all times to any parent in need of guidance, with emphasis on the well-being of the children; sixth, to cooperate with other institutions and organisations on matters of mutual interest; and, seventh, to provide single parents with a sense of belonging in a two-parent society.

- Single Parent Information Network (SPIN; see: http://spinbrighton. shutterfly.com/): SPIN is a free information and signposting organisation based in Brighton, East Sussex. SPIN started in 2005 and is a constituted voluntary organisation. The organisation was set up by the current Director as a result of her own experiences as a single parent and a lack of information to improve her quality of life given her circumstances. SPIN's main focus is to provide information to single parents by single-parent volunteers and to improve the quality of life of single-parent families. Moreover, SPIN aims: to provide a network via an Internet group, social events and projects to increase access, opportunities and reduce isolation; to provide volunteer opportunities that will increase member skills and confidence; and to run projects/events of benefit to members and volunteers.

- One Family (see: http://www.onefamily.ie/about-us/): One Family is Ireland's national organisation for one-parent families. One Family works with all types and all members of one-parent families to effect positive change and achieve equality and social inclusion for all one-parent families in Ireland. One Family offers support, information and services to all members of all one-parent families, to those experiencing an unplanned pregnancy and to those working with one-parent families. The organisation puts children at the centre of its work. One Family's holistic model of family support services works in two ways: first, to progress parents on social welfare to take the next step to education, training or employment; and, second, to provide expert parenting and family supports to people parenting alone or sharing parenting and to those working with one-parent families.

- Single Mothers by Choice (SMC; see: http://www. singlemothersbychoice.org/): an organisation founded in 1981 by Jane Mattes, LCSW, a psychotherapist and single mother by choice. Single Mothers by Choice's primary purpose is to provide support and information to single women who are considering, or have chosen, single motherhood. Members meet with one another all over the US, and in Canada, Europe and beyond. They share information and resources about donor insemination, adoption and parenting at local levels and/or through a lively online discussion forum and newsletters.

• Project Single Moms Worldwide (PSM; see: http://www. projectsinglemoms.com/blog1/?page_id=301): the PSM website community is based in Atlanta (Georgia, US). Through strategic partnerships with individuals, corporations, faith and community-based organisations, and government agencies, PSM works to create opportunities to strengthen and enhance the quality of life for single mothers and their families. PSM focuses its efforts on identifying and creating opportunities for single mothers in the following eight core empowerment areas: advanced education; employment; parenting skills and support; financial literary and wealth-building; health and wellness (mental, emotional, spiritual and physical); home-ownership attainment; starting and growing a successful business; and personal empowerment and self-development. The PSM empowerment movement is driven and led by working single mothers who volunteer their time and talents to lead the movement. The movement welcomes individuals who are not single mothers to serve in these capacities in support of the movement.

Notes

[1] The 20-year fascist period (*Ventennio fascista*), under the leadership of Benito Mussolini, ran from 1922 to 1943. See the introductory chapter for details.

[2] The 'Research report on the situation of lone parents in Supermom partner countries' can be downloaded in the partner languages and is intended to serve as an overview of the situation of single parents in each Supermom partner country: Italy, Germany, Poland, France and the UK (Northern Ireland). The reports gives an insight into key areas, such as demographics, modes and availability of childcare, social welfare benefits, employment and education levels of lone parents, and poverty among one-parent families (see: http://www.supermom-kick-off.eu/single-parents-in-europe/index. php). (All websites cited in this chapter have been consulted in the period September–December 2012.)

[3] The General Lifestyle Survey, formerly known as the General Household Survey (GHS), is a multi-purpose continuous survey carried out by the Office for National Statistics (ONS) to collect information on a range of topics from people living in private households in Great Britain. This information is used by government departments and other organisations for planning, policy and

monitoring purposes and to present a picture of households, family and people in Great Britain (see: http://www.esds.ac.uk/government/ghs/).

[4] See: http://www.gingerbreadni.org/

[5] See: http://library.wlu.edu/details.php?resID=114 and http://www.encyclopedia.com/topic/Single-Parent_Families.aspx

[6] See: http://www.encyclopedia.com/topic/Single-Parent_Families.aspx

[7] See: http://family.jrank.org/pages/1574/Single-Parent-Families-Demographic-Trends.html

[8] See: http://www.ined.fr/en/everything_about_population/faq/marriage_famille/bdd/q_text/how_many_children_in_france_live_in_a_single_parent_family_/question/217/

[9] See: http://www.dailymail.co.uk/news/article-2089144/Britain-million-single-parent-families-majority-children-raised-mother-alone.html

[10] See: http://www.abs.gov.au/ausstats/abs@.nsf/0/F4B15709EC89CB1EC A25732C002079B2?opendocument

[11] See: http://www.abs.gov.au/ausstats/abs@.nsf/0/F4B15709EC89CB1EC A25732C002079B2?opendocument

[12] See: http://library.wlu.edu/details.php?resID=114 and http://www.encyclopedia.com/topic/Single-Parent_Families.aspx

[13] The ECHP is a panel survey in which a sample of households and persons has been interviewed year after year. These interviews cover a wide range of topics concerning living conditions. They include detailed information on the income, financial situations in a wider sense, working life, housing situations, social relations, health and biographies of the interviewed. The total duration of the ECHP was eight years, running from 1994 to 2001 (eight waves) (see: http://epp.eurostat.ec.europa.eu/portal/page/portal/microdata/echp).

[14] See: http://www.ons.gov.uk/ons/rel/family-demography/families-and-households/2011/stb-families-households.html#tab-Lone-parents

[15] See: http://www.abs.gov.au/ausstats/abs@.nsf/0/F4B15709EC89CB1EC A25732C002079B2?opendocument

[16] The EU-SILC aims at collecting comparable cross-sectional and longitudinal multidimensional microdata on income, poverty, social exclusion and living conditions. The EU-SILC project was launched in 2003 in six member states (Belgium, Denmark, Greece, Ireland, Luxembourg and Austria), as well as in Norway. The EU-SILC provides two types of annual data for 27 EU countries plus Croatia, Iceland, Norway, Switzerland and Turkey: first, cross-sectional data pertaining to a given time or a certain time period with variables on income, poverty, social exclusion and other living conditions; and, second, longitudinal data pertaining to individual-level changes over time, observed periodically over a four-year period (see: http://epp.eurostat.ec.europa.eu/portal/page/portal/microdata/eu_silc).

[17] See: http://www.combatpoverty.ie/povertyinireland/oneparentfamilies.htm

[18] For details about the BHPS, see Chapter Three, note 4.

[19] Support networks are different for men and women, as are the resources available for men and women, relating to their education level and the social class they belong to (Piselli, 2000).

[20] See: http://www.buzzle.com/articles/single-parenting-effects.html and http://lifestyle.iloveindia.com/lounge/single-parenting-effects-11544.html

References

ABS-Australian Bureau of Statistics (2006) 'Fathers' work and family balance', 4102.0 *Australian Social Trends*. Available at: http://www.abs.gov.au/ausstats/abs@.nsf/bb8db737e2af84b8ca2571780015701e/acf29854f8c8509eca2571b00010329b!OpenDocument

Acock, A.C. and Demo, D.H. (1994) *Family diversity and well-being*, Thousand Oaks, CA: Sage.

Albelda, R., Himmelweit, S. and Humphries, J. (eds) (2005) *Dilemmas of lone motherhood*, London and New York, NY: Routledge.

Amato, P.R. (2000a) 'Diversity within single-parent families', in D. Demo, K.R. Allen and M.A. Fine (eds) *Handbook of family diversity*, New York, NY: Oxford University Press, pp 149–72.

Amato, P.R. (2000b) 'The consequences of divorce for adults and children', *Journal of Marriage and Family*, vol 62, no 4, pp 1269–87.

Amato, P.R. and Booth, A. (1997) *A generation at risk: growing up in an era of family upheaval*, Cambridge, MA: Harvard University Press.

Baker, D. and North, K. (1999) 'Does employment improve the health of lone mothers?', *Social Science and Medicine*, vol 49, no 1, pp 121–32.

Beatson, K., Davey, C. and Scott, S. (2011) 'Single parent families'. Available at: http://www.anthonygold.co.uk/site/ang_articles/single_parent_families_kim_beatson

Beaupré, P., Dryburgh, H. and Wendt, M. (2010) 'Making fathers "count"', Canadian Social Trends, Statistics Canada. Available at: http://www.statcan.gc.ca/pub/11-008-x/2010002/article/11165-eng.htm

Benzeval, M. (1998) 'The self-reported health status of lone parents', *Social Science and Medicine*, vol 46, pp 1337–53.

Berthoud, R. and Robson, K. (2001) *The outcomes of teenage motherhood in Europe*, EPAG Working Paper 22, Colchester: University of Essex.

Bimbi, F. (1997) 'Lone mothers in Italy. A hidden and embarrassing issue in a familist welfare regime', in J. Lewis (ed) *Lone mothers in European welfare regimes: Shifting policy logics*, London and Philadelphia, PA: Jessica Kingsley Publishers.

Bimbi, F. (ed) (2000) *Madri sole. Metafore della famiglia ed esclusione sociale* [*Lone mothers: Family metaphors and social exclusion*], Roma: Carocci.

Bradbury, B., Jenkins, S. and Micklewright, J. (2001) 'Beyond the snapshot: a dynamic view of child poverty', in B. Bradbury, S. Jenkins and J. Micklewright (eds) *The dynamics of child poverty in industrialised countries*, New York, NY: Cambridge University Press, pp 1–26.

Caballero, C. and Edwards, R. (2010) 'Lone mothers of children from mixed racial and ethnic: here and now', Runnymede Perspectives Series. Available at: http://www.runnymedetrust.org/uploads/publications/pdfs/LoneMothers-2010.pdf

Cliquet, R. (2003) 'Major trends affecting families in the new millennium. Western Europe and North America', in United Nations (ed) *Major trends affecting families. A background document*, New York, NY: United Nations, pp 1–26. Available at: http://www.un.org/esa/socdev/family/Publications/mtcliquet.pdf and http://social.un.org/index/Family/Publications/MajorTrendsAffectingFamilies.aspx

Combat Poverty Agency (2006) 'Lone parent families and poverty'. Available at: http://www.cpa.ie/publications/factsheets/Factsheet_LoneParents.pdf

Coontz, S. (1997) *The way we really are: coming to terms with America's changing families*, New York, NY: Basic Books.

Cunnington, A.J. (2001) 'What's so bad about teenage pregnancy?', *Journal of Family Planning and Reproductive Health Care*, vol 21, no 1, pp 36–41.

Daguerre, A. and Nativel, C. (eds) (2008) *When children become parents. Welfare state responses to teenage pregnancy*, Bristol: The Policy Press.

De Grazia,V. (1992) *How fascism ruled women 1922–1943*, Berkeley, CA: University of California Press.

DeLeire, T. and Kalil, A. (2001) 'Good things come in threes: single-parent multigenerational family structure and adolescent adjustment', Harris Graduate School of Public Policy Studies, University of Chicago, October. Available at: http://www.ipr.northwestern.edu/jcpr/workingpapers/wpfiles/deleire_kalil.pdf

Demo, D.H. and Acock, A.C. (1991) 'The impact of divorce on children', in A. Booth (ed) *Contemporary families: looking forward, looking back*, Minneapolis, MN: National Council on Family Relations, pp 162–91.

Duncan, S. and Edwards, R. (eds) (1997) *Single mothers in international context; mothers or workers?*, London: UCL Press.

Edin, K. and Lein, L. (1997) *Making ends meet: how single mothers survive welfare and low-wage work*, New York, NY: Russel Sage Foundation.

Feltey K.M. (2003) 'Single-parent families', in James J. Ponzetti Jr. (ed), *The international encyclopedia of marriage and family* (2nd edn), NY: Macmillan Reference USA, pp 1515-23.

Flood, M. (2007) 'Supporting separated fathers and encouraging men's positive involvement in parenting', The Field of Fatherhood: Crossings of the Terrain, Conference, Hawke Institute for Sustainable Societies, University of South Australia. Available at: http://www.cpa.ie/publications/factsheets/Factsheet_LoneParents.pdf

Fraser, A.M., Brockert, J.E. and Ward, R.H. (1995) 'Association of young maternal age with adverse reproductive outcomes', *New England Journal of Medicine*, vol 332, no 17, pp 1113–17.

Glicken, M.D. (2013) *Social work in the 21st century, an introduction to social welfare, social issues, and the profession* (2nd edn), London: Sage. Available at: http://www.sagepub.com/glicken2e/study/chapter.htm and http://www.sagepub.com/upm-data/38142_Chapter2.pdf

Gongla, P.A. (1982) 'Single-parent families: a look at families of mothers and children', *Marriage and Family Review*, vol 5, no 2, pp 5–27.

González, L. (2008) 'A decomposition of the incidence of single mothers in Europe', Universitat Pompeu Fabra, November. Available at: http://www.econ.upf.edu/~gonzalez/Research_archivos/November_2008.pdf

Greif, G.L. (1992) 'Lone fathers in the United States: an overview and practice implications', *British Journal of Social Work*, vol 22, no 5, pp 565–74.

Haddon, L. (2000) 'Social exclusion and information and communication technologies. Lessons from studies of single parents and the young elderly', *New Media & Society*, vol 2, no 4, pp 387–406. Available at: http://rcirib.ir/articles/pdfs/cd1%5CIngenta_Sage_Articles_on_194_225_11_89/Ingenta764.pdf

Haddon, L. and Silverstone, R. (1994) 'Lone parents and their information and communication technologies', SPRU CICT Report Series no 12, November, University of Sussex. Available at: http://www2.lse.ac.uk/media@lse/whosWho/AcademicStaff/LeslieHaddon/LONEREP.pdf

Hertz, R. (2006) *Single by chance, mothers by choice. How women are choosing parenthood without marriage and creating the new American family*, New York, NY: Oxford University Press.

Hobson, B. (1994) 'Solo mothers, social policy regimes and the logics of gender', in D. Sainsbury (ed) *Gendering welfare states*, London: Sage Publications, pp 170–87.

Huda, P.R. (2001) 'Singled out: a critique of the representation of single motherhood in welfare discourse', *William & Mary Journal of Women and the Law*, vol 7, nos 2/3, pp 341–81. Available at: http://scholarship.law.wm.edu/wmjowl

Kertzer, D. (1993) *Sacrificed for honor: Italian infant abandonment and the politics of reproductive control*, Boston, MA: Beacon Press.

Klett-Davies, M. (2007) *Going it alone? Lone motherhood in late modernity*, Aldershot: Ashgate.

Lamb, M.E. (ed) (2004) *The role of the father in child development* (4th edn), Hoboken, NJ: John Wiley & Sons.

Larkin, M. (2009) *Vulnerable groups in health and social care*, London: Sage Publications.

Leccardi, C. and Ruspini, E. (eds) (2006) *A new youth? Young people, generations and family life*, Aldershot: Ashgate Publishing.

Lewis, J. (ed) (1997) *Lone mothers in European welfare regimes: shifting policy logics*, London: Jessica Kingsley Publisher.

Marsden, D. (1969) *Mothers alone: poverty and the fatherless family*, London: Allen Lane.

Mata, F. (2011) 'Lone parent status among ethnic groups in Canada: census data explorations on its prevalence, composition and generational persistence aspects', Metropolis British Columbia, Centre of Excellence for Research on Immigration and Diversity, Working Paper Series, Paper no 11-17, November. Available at: http://www.mbc.metropolis.net/assets/uploads/files/wp/2011/WP11-17.pdf

Mauldin, T.A. (1990) 'Women who remain above the poverty level in divorce: implications for family policy', *Family Relations*, vol 39, no 2, pp 141–6.

McLanahan, S. and Booth, K. (1989) 'Mother-only families: problems, prospects, and politics', *Journal of Marriage and the Family*, vol 5, no 3, pp 557–80.

McLanahan, S. and Sandefur, G. (1994) *Growing up with a single parent: what hurts, what helps*, Cambridge, MA: Harvard University Press.

Millar, J. and Ridge, T. (2001) 'Families, poverty, work and care: a review of the literature on lone parents and low-income couple families with children', Centre for the Analysis of Social Policy at the University of Bath and Department for Work and Pensions, Research Report no 153. Available at: http://statistics.dwp.gov.uk/asd/asd5/rrep153.pdf

Millar, J. and Rowlingson, K. (eds) (2001) *Lone parents, employment and social policy: Cross-national comparisons*, Bristol: The Policy Press.

Miller, N. (1992) *Single parents by choice. A growing trend in family life*, New York, NY: Insight Books.

National Council for One Parent Families (1999) *One parent families today: the facts – a summary report from the National Council for One parent Families*, London: National Council for One Parent Families.

ONS (Office for National Statistics) (2007) 'Social trends', no 37, A. Self and L. Zealey (eds) . Available at: http://news.bbc.co.uk/2/shared/bsp/hi/pdfs/11_04_07_social_trends.pdf

Pedersen, L., Weise, H., Jacobs, S. and White, M. (2000) 'Lone mothers' poverty and employment', in D. Gallie and S. Paugam (eds) *Welfare regimes and the experience of unemployment in Europe*, New York, NY: Oxford University Press, pp 175–99.

Piselli, F. (2000) 'La network analysis' ['Network analysis'], paper presented at the Workshop 'Genere e ricerca sociale: una sfida per la sociologia italiana' ('Gender and social research. A challenge for Italian sociology'), University of Milano-Bicocca, Milan, June.

Popay, J. and Jones, G. (1990) 'Patterns of health and illness amongst lone parents', *Journal of Social Policy*, vol 19, no 4, pp 499–534.

Pruett, K.D. (2000) *Fatherneed: why father care is as essential as mother care for your child*, New York, NY: The Free Press.

Rodgers, H.R., Jr (1996) *Poor women, poor children: American poverty in the 1990s*, Armonk, NY: M.E. Sharpe.

Roll, J. (ed) (1992) *Lone parent families in the European Community. The 1992 report to the European Commission*, Brussels: Commission of the European Communities, Equal Opportunities Unit.

Rosenberg, J. and Bradford, W.W. (2006) 'The importance of fathers in the healthy development of children', Office on Child Abuse and Neglect, US Children's Bureau. Available at: https://www.childwelfare.gov/pubs/usermanuals/fatherhood/chaptertwo.cfm

Rowlingson, K. (2001) 'The social, economic and demographic profile of lone parents', in J. Millar and K. Rowlingson (eds) *Lone parents, employment and social policy. Cross-national comparison*, Bristol: The Policy Press.

Rowlingson, K. and McKay, S. (1998) *The growth of lone parenthood: diversity and dynamics*, London: Policy Studies Institute.

Rowlingson, K. and McKay, S. (2005) 'Lone motherhood and socio-economic disadvantage: insights from quantitative and qualitative evidence', *The Sociological Review*, vol 53, no 1, pp 30–49.

Ruspini, E. (2001) 'Lone mothers' poverty in Europe: the cases of Belgium, Germany, Great Britain, Italy and Sweden', in A. Pfenning and T. Bahle (eds) *Families and family policies in Europe. Comparative perspectives*, Frankfurt am Main and New York, NY: Peter Lang, pp 221–44.

Ruspini, E. (2006) 'Going against the tide. Young lone mothers in Italy', in C. Leccardi and E. Ruspini (eds) *A new youth? Young people, generations and family life*, Aldershot: Ashgate Publishing, pp 253–75.

Ruspini, E. (2010) *Monoparentalité, homoparentalité, transparentalité en France et en Italie. Tendances, défis et nouvelles exigences*, Collection 'Logiques Sociales', Paris: L'Harmattan.

Sands, R.G. and Nuccio, K.E. (1989) 'Mother-headed single-parent families: a feminist perspective', *Affilia*, vol 4, pp 25–41.

Scheiwe, K. (1994) 'Labour market, welfare state and family institutions: the links to mothers' poverty risks. A comparison between Belgium, Germany and the United Kingdom', *Journal of European Social Policy*, vol 4, no 3, pp 201–24.

Simoni, S. (2000) 'La costruzione di un'assenza nella storia del sistema italiano di welfare' ['The social construction of an absence in the Italian welfare state'], in F. Bimbi (ed) *Madri sole. Metafore della famiglia ed esclusione sociale*, Roma: Carocci, pp 85–100.

Singh, S. and Darroch, J.E. (2000) 'Adolescent pregnancy and childbearing: levels and trends in developed countries', *Family Planning Perspectives*, vol 32, no 1, pp 14–23.

Skevik, A. (2001) 'Family ideology and social policy. Policies towards lone parents in Norway and the UK', Norwegian Social Research, Rapport 7.

Stanley, F., Richardson, S. and Prior, M. (2005) *Children of the lucky country? How Australian society has turned its back on children and why children matter*, Sydney: Macmillan Australia.

Swain, S. and Howe, R. (1995) *Single mothers and their children: disposal, punishment and survival in Australia*, New York, NY: Cambridge University Press.

Terragni, L. (2000) 'Le madri nubili e i loro figli illegittimi: la ridefinizione di un ruolo sociale tra Ottocento e Novecento' ['Non-married mothers and their "illegitimate" children between the 19th and 20th centuries'], in F. Bimbi (ed) *Madri sole. Metafore della famiglia ed esclusione sociale*, Roma: Carocci, pp 75–84.

Tokoro, M. (2003) 'Social policy and lone parenthood in Japan: a workfare tradition?', *The Japanese Journal of Social Security Policy*, vol 2, no 2. Available at: http://www.ipss.go.jp/webj-ad/webjournal.files/socialsecurity/2003/03dec/Tokoro2003dec.pdf

CHAPTER SIX

Homosexual and trans parents

Homosexual and transgender parenting

In this chapter, we examine a selection of research findings on the characteristics, advantages and drawbacks of homosexual and transgender parenting experiences. The phenomenon of *homosexual parenting* (also ***homo-parenthood***[1] – a term that includes all those families in which at least one adult who defines him/herself as homosexual is the parent of at least one child (Nadaud, 2002; Gross, 2003) – has for some time now been an emerging reality in many Western societies, above all following the growing visibility of homosexual mothers living with their partners and their children. Homosexual parenting must be observed from several angles. We must not only consider the desire for motherhood or fatherhood in gays and lesbians, but also the paternal and maternal responsibility of all those homosexuals who have 'procreated' in their previous heterosexual relationships. Lesbian and gay parents and their children are a diverse group.

Equally topical and important is the relationship between parenthood, **transgenderism** (please see **transgender** in the Glossary) and **transsexuality**. We may speak of *transgender parenting* (also *trans parenting*) when at least one adult, the mother or father of at least one child, decides to make the transition from one gender to the other.[2] Transition is the process through which a person modifies his/her physical characteristics and/or manner of expression to satisfy the standards for membership in a gender other than the one assigned at birth. Transitioning may include changing one's name, taking hormones, having surgery or changing legal documents (eg driver's licence, Social Security record, birth certificate) to reflect their new gender. Also in the case of trans parenting, we must both consider the desire for children in transgender persons, and the paternal and maternal responsibility of all those persons who already have children.

In our opinion, addressing homosexual and transgender parenting poses a major challenge to contemporary scholarship; it requires an analysis of the experience of **intimacy** within the context of **sexual orientation** and gender transition, a consideration of the impact of gender transition upon partnering relationships, and a recognition of the ways in which sexual orientation and gender transition are negotiated within parenting relationships (Hines, 2006). At the same time, however, the incorporation of homosexual and transgender parenting experiences into analyses of contemporary practices of intimacy enables a richer understanding of wider social changes in family life.

Although the American Psychiatric Association de-pathologised homosexuality in 1973 by removing it from the list of psychological disorders in the Diagnostic and Statistical Manual of Mental Disorders (DSM), now in its fourth edition (DSM-IV),[3] and the American Psychological Association acted similarly in 1975, some psychologists have remained resistant to the new perspective (Fontaine and Hammond, 1996). For example, a survey of psychologists reported 12 years after the DSM-IV was published found that nearly 30% of responding clinicians felt that treating homosexuality per se as pathological constituted ethical practice (Pope et al, 1987).

As Guidotto (2005) notes, 'transsexual' was not really considered a pronounced subjectivity until the late 19th and early 20th centuries, when medical practitioners and sexologists set out to distinguish different types of human behaviour. The resulting term 'homosexual inversion' conflated gender variance with sexual orientation (Sullivan, 2003, p 4). By the latter part of the 19th century, however, gender variance was distinguished from homosexuality and redefined as 'transsexuality' (Halberstam, 1998). The diagnosis of transsexualism was included in the DSM-III in 1980. The DSM-III defined transsexuals as gender dysphoric individuals who show and feel persistent discomfort with their **gender identity** and associated gender and social roles, and who demonstrated at least two years of continuous interest in removing their sexual anatomy and transforming their bodies and social roles.[4] Unlike homosexuality, transsexuality continues to be regarded as a pathological condition by the American Psychiatric Association. In 1994, the DSM-IV committee replaced the diagnosis of transsexualism with 'gender identity disorder'. Depending on their age, those with a strong and persistent cross-gender identification and a persistent discomfort with their sex or a sense of inappropriateness in the **gender role** of that sex are seen as having a gender identity disorder (of childhood, adolescence or adulthood), and transsexuality is often attributed to 'abnormal' psychological development.

Research on homosexual parenting

The experience of being parents and having relationships with persons of the same sex is obviously not new, but a number of studies (especially in the United States and in Great Britain) describe major changes (Miller et al, 1981; Green et al, 1986; Bozett, 1987 and 1989; Bozett and Sussman, 1990; Tasker and Golombok, 1997; Stacey, 2002; Stacey and Biblarz, 2001; Bos et al, 2004; Mallon, 2004; Gratton, 2008; Ruspini, 2010b). While the children of homosexual parents generally came from a previous heterosexual relationship in the past, with the possibilities opened up by **assisted reproductive technology** and increased access to adoption, the decision to become a parent now is increasingly disconnected from heterosexuality (Shanley, 2002; Bertone, 2005).

The contemporary homosexual family is the result of a complex series of choices (Gross, 2003; Goldberg and Allen, 2013):

- the reforming of a family with a partner of the same sex after a heterosexual union;
- a system of co-parenthood within which gays and lesbians agree to have a child that will be brought up in the two families;
- a 'hetero-gay family', which is a relatively new family configuration that is headed by a heterosexual mother and gay father who conceive and raise children together, although residing separately (Segal-Engelchin et al, 2005);
- an adoption (forbidden by law for homosexual couples in countries such as Austria, Italy[5] and Poland);
- artificial insemination (AI) for lesbian couples, which is a process whereby donated semen is inserted into a female for the purpose of fertilisation by means other than ejaculation. It involves preparing and placing sperm directly into the cervical canal or the reproductive tract of the woman and does not involve sexual intercourse. The most commonly used method of artificial insemination, is Intrauterine Insemination (IUI);[6]
- medically assisted procreation; and
- **surrogate motherhood**, where one woman acts as a surrogate, or replacement, mother for another woman.

How many children live in homosexual families? According to estimates made by the *Institut National d'Etudes Démographiques* (National Institute of Demographic Studies; INED),[7] some 30,000 children in France already live in a family nucleus composed of two adults of the same sex. In Italy, there are approximately 100,000 children with homosexual parents. The findings of a research study carried out in 2005 by *Arcigay* (the Italian Lesbian and Gay Association) with the support of the *Istituto Superiore di Sanità* (Higher Institute for Health), show that 17.7% of Italian gay men and 20.5% of lesbians over the age of 40 have at least one child. In Australia, the 2001 Census identified 11,000 male same-sex couples and 9,000 female same-sex couples. Nationally, same-sex couple families tended to be smaller than opposite-sex couple families, with an average number of residents of 2.1 for female same-sex couples, 2.3 for male same-sex couples and 3.2 for opposite-sex couples in 2001. The proportion of families without children was also higher for same-sex couples, at 95% of male same-sex couples and 81% of female same-sex couples, compared with 43% for opposite-sex couples. Of the couples with children, a higher proportion of same-sex couples had only one child (49% of male same-sex couples and 54% of female same-sex couples, compared with 34% of opposite-sex couples). Finally, statistics from the 2000 US Census, the 2002 National Survey of Family Growth (NSFG)[8] and the 2004 Adoption and Foster Care Analysis and Reporting System (AFCARS)[9] show that an estimated 65,500 adopted children are living with a lesbian or gay parent nationwide, and more than 16,000 adopted children are living with lesbian and gay parents in California (the highest number among the states). Strikingly, gay and lesbian parents are raising 4% of all adopted children in the US, and adopted children with same-sex parents are younger and more likely to be foreign-born.[10]

Yet, across the world, gays, lesbians and transsexuals are subject to open discrimination as far as their rights to parenthood are concerned. They are also plagued by negative stereotypes, for example: 'In order to grow up properly, a child needs a father and a mother'; 'Male homosexual relations are less stable than heterosexual ones and therefore do not guarantee family continuity'; 'Gays are paedophiles'; 'Gay fathers are likely to carry HIV/AIDS and infect children with HIV/AIDS'; 'The children of homosexual people have more psychological problems than those of heterosexuals'; and 'The children of homosexuals are more likely to become homosexual' (Ruspini, 2010a).

However, comparative studies suggest that children with gay and lesbian parents do not differ from children with heterosexual parents in their emotional development or in their relationships with peers and adults. The earliest of these studies, conducted by Scallen (1982), compared gay fathers and heterosexual fathers by means of a questionnaire aimed at defining parental skills. Gay fathers proved to be more supportive of children and, at the same time, less traditionalist in their views of parenthood. A well-known study by Golombok, Spencer and Rutter (1983) had similar findings. Thirty-seven school-age children reared in 27 lesbian households were compared with 38 school-age children reared in 27 heterosexual single-parent households, with respect to their psychosexual development and their emotions, behaviour and relationships. Systematic standardised interviews with the mothers and with the children, together with parent and teacher questionnaires, were employed in order to make a psychosexual and psychiatric appraisal. The two groups did not differ in terms of gender identity, sex role behaviour or sexual orientation. Also, they did not differ on most measures of emotions, behaviour and relationships – although there was some indication of more frequent psychiatric problems in the single-parent group. It was concluded that rearing in a lesbian household per se did not lead to atypical psychosexual development. For Harris and Turner (1985/86), homosexuality is not at all incompatible with carrying out the paternal role. No difference has been found between heterosexual and homosexual fathers concerning problem-solving (the set of processes aimed at analysing, dealing with and positively solving problematic situations), play activities and the encouragement of independence, and no difficulties emerged in carrying out care functions. Gay fathers also proved to be less authoritarian and more attentive to the needs of their children.

Similarly, in a study by Bigner and Jacobsen (1989) on 33 homosexual fathers and 33 heterosexual resident in Iowa, the two groups showed no difference regarding the level of involvement or intimacy with their children. On the contrary, the homosexual fathers appeared more attentive to their children's needs and more willing to understand the younger generations. Moreover, Bailey et al (1995) – in a broad study on the orientation of sexual conduct of 55 gay or bisexual men (with a total of 83 male children aged at least 17, subsequently contacted by the research group) recruited through ads in gay magazines – show that in 90% of cases, the children described themselves as heterosexual.

Lastly, a very recent study by Charlotte Patterson (2006) suggests that parental sexual orientation has no significant impact on child or adolescent development. Patterson concludes that parental sexual orientation is less important than the quality of family relationships, the character of daily interaction and the strength of relationships with the parents they have. All in all, the existing research show that children's health and well-being are not linked to the sexual orientation of their parents: the children brought up by gay and lesbian couples are equally likely to grow up well as those brought up by heterosexual couples (for a synthesis, see Bottino and Danna, 2005).

The situation for gay fathers is rather more complicated than for lesbian mothers. To begin with, research on gay fathers and their children is still limited in extent; although studies of gay fathers and their children have been conducted (see, eg, Patterson and Redding, 1996; Patterson, 2004, 2005), less is known about the children of gay fathers than about the children of lesbian mothers.

Moreover, many fathers are impacted (both personally and in social relationships) by negative stereotypes about gay men and parenting, and researchers have found that gay fathers identify many complex issues related to **coming out** with children and spouses, including fear of the children's and spouse's homophobia. Some of the men (especially if they had children in the context of a previous heterosexual relationship) were struggling with a newly acquired gay identity and the integration of this with their identity as a parent (Epstein and Duggan, 2006).

And, indeed, gay men who have children face many challenges after coming out. Research (Buxton, 2009) shows that children may express a variety of concerns in relation to the coming out of their fathers. Some children say that they are embarrassed by any changes in their parent's appearance or interactions with gay friends or a partner. Many fear that their father will be infected by the AIDS virus. Other feel hurt by anti-gay attitudes expressed by friends, neighbours or classmates. Moreover, each age brings its particular reactions and expressed needs. Young children, not knowing much about sexual orientation, take the announcement as a matter of fact, as long as they are assured that both parents continue to love them and will be there for them. Older, school-age children may fear taunts from classmates. Teenagers, whose own sexuality is emerging, have probably the hardest time accepting the news. And, of course, a woman who discovers that her husband/partner is a homosexual also faces many difficulties.

Most significant are the complexities involved in acquiring children (through adoption, surrogacy or co-parenting arrangements). Given the difficulty of adoption and of access to assisted reproduction techniques, gay male couples have very limited opportunities to live together and bring up a child. A gay man may, for example, make an agreement with a lesbian couple to construct a three-parent, or (with a partner) four-person co-parenting, family. He may offer to be a donor of non-anonymous sperm, asking to maintain limited contact with the offspring. He may seek out a foreign partner willing to adopt a child in his country of origin, where this is possible. Another possibility is surrogate motherhood, the practice whereby a woman agrees to undergo a pregnancy in the place of another person. Finally, gay men who wish to rear a child together may face additional problems if they have children from a previous heterosexual relationship.

One thing appears clear. For the children, the difficulty does not seem to be their parents' sexual preference, but societal attitudes regarding that preference. Children growing up and living in homosexual families have to struggle more against stigmatisation, discrimination and bullying (see, eg, Ray and Gregory, 2001). These findings indicate that homophobia and transphobia, that is, expressions of repulsion, fear and/or contempt for homosexual, bisexual, transgender and transsexual persons, are likely the main reason why the sexual preferences of parents may negatively affect their children.

Research on transgender parenting

A set of recent studies found that up to one third of transsexuals attending a gender identity clinic had children, but the number of children attending a gender identity clinic who have at least one transsexual parent is small. This suggests that a parent's gender transition is not a significant influence on a child's sexual development (Freedman et al, 2002).

However, the literature dealing with transgender parenting and family dynamics is limited. Moreover, as Bischof et al (2011) note, much of the literature emphasises the negative aspects (eg depression, family issues, job/career challenges) of transitioning on couples and families; yet, there are potential positive aspects and strengths (eg being more true to self, resiliency, positive identity changes) of these couples that should be highlighted (Israel, 2004).

For example, it is generally thought that the transsexuality of one of the parents may be a source of malaise and suffering for their children, most notably, that the transsexuality of a parent might have harmful effects on the child's development (Luciani, 2010). Given those concerns, when a partner or spouse comes out as a transsexual, the parents may decide to separate in order to prevent negative developmental outcomes. But the progressive distancing of the father or mother who is making the transition may well create more problems than it solves.

Transsexuals also face major problems with regard to both national and international adoption. Although suitability for adoptive parenthood ought to be assessed according to standard criteria unanimously recognised and applied, a request put forward by a regularly married couple, in which one of the partners has undergone surgical and personal data reassignment is normally refused. In Italy, for example, the rejection is justified by Law 184/83 and the subsequent modifications of Law 149/01 (which govern adoption and fostering). Moreover, according to current law in Italy, once the application for sexual reassignment is ratified by a competent law court, a husband and wife may not stay married. At the same time, the judge pronouncing the sentence of divorce has the power to prevent the transsexual partner from exercising parental power over the child, above all, in cases when factors of 'evolutionary risk' are perceived. Faced with this delicate task, and in order to act in the best interests of the child, the judge often rules based on two implicit and widely accepted convictions: first, that the child is not able to understand and follow the parent's change; and, second, that the transsexual parent is no longer able to carry out the role of a mother/father. Such attitudes have been criticised since no tangible evidence exists to support the idea that the transformation of anatomical appearance and gender identity may affect one's ability to carry out those parental functions that, we may recall, have accompanied the child since their birth (Luciani, 2010).

Published research examining the psychosocial development of children of transsexual parents is not rich. However, available evidence does not support concerns that a parent's transsexuality has a direct and adverse impact on their children. By contrast, however, there is extensive clinical experience showing the detrimental consequences for children who have little or no contact with a parent after divorce (Green, 1978, 1998; Freedman et al, 2002).

Green (1978) studied 37 children raised by lesbian or transsexual parents and, comparing them to children raised in heteronormative settings, found no significant differences. Although data were not systematically recorded on key aspects of the children's experience with respect to parenting and family relationships, peer relationships, or mental health, none of the 16 children (aged from three to 20 years old) of the seven transsexual parents in his study had gender identity problems and all reported gender-typical activities and interests.[11] All of the 13 post-pubertal children reported heterosexual fantasies and relationships.

Yet, clinical reports do suggest that sex reassignment treatments bring into question the existing patterns of relating between the parent and child (Sales, 1995; Lightfoot, 1998). Studies indicate that there are two primary factors that predict a healthier or less-conflicted relationship between the child and the transitioning and non-transitioning parent: the age of the child at the time of the transition; and a positive relationship between the two parents. As White and Ettner (2004) note, younger children adjust much better to the transition than adolescents and young adults. Adolescents show the greatest difficulties adjusting;

this is especially true when considerable family conflict exists or divorce occurs.

The better the relationship between the transitioning parent and the child was prior to transition, the better the long-term relationship. As is true for children of divorce, children who experience considerable parental conflict tend to have greater difficulties in adjustment (White and Ettner, 2004). Notably, children and adolescents who experience greater stress tend to have greater difficulties in academic performance – a common measure of childhood adjustment. However, while there is a relationship between decline in academic performance and level of family conflict in situations involving divorce, that has not been found to be the case when a parent was transitioning. Although there may be considerable conflict between the parents at the time of the transition, this does not negatively impact the child, unless the conflict persists over time (White and Ettner, 2004).

Of course, transition has an impact on every aspect of life of the trans person (Tully, 1992; King, 1993), and the many changes and adjustments may relate directly to the parenting of children. For instance, the transsexual parent may be preoccupied with bodily and psychological changes and find it difficult to appreciate their son's or daughter's difficulty in accepting and adjusting to the change. The child may also not know how to refer to their parent in different social contexts and whether (or how) to explain their parent's situation to others. The seeking of sex reassignment treatment brings the parent into contact with adult clinical services, potentially influencing the way that the transsexual parent, the non-transsexual parent and their children handle issues connected with their parents' identity.

Transsexual parents may profit from engaging with children in counselling sessions in anticipation of, or during, the gender transition process, where concerns and questions can be addressed. Marital counselling early in the transition process may mitigate the hostility of the non-transsexual parent. Children can also benefit from counselling after parental sex reassignment (Sales, 1995). One decision that families face is what name to use for the parent post-transition, and one third of the children continue to use the pre-transition gender-specific identifier (ie 'mom' for a female-to-male transition). Following White and Ettner (2007), those children who use the pre-transition parent identifier, or those who have no contact with their parent, are those who are most embarrassed by the transition. Children who are not embarrassed by the transition adopt either their parent's first name, a neutral nickname or a post-transition gender-congruent title (ie 'mom' or 'dad').

The homosexual and trans parents rights movement

In order to end discrimination and to secure equal civil rights for homosexual and trans families, many associations, websites and networks have been created:

- Parents, Families and Friends of Lesbians and Gays (PFLAG)[12] is a non-profit organisation with over 200,000 members and supporters and over 350 affiliates in the US and is one of the largest of these groups. This vast network is cultivated, resourced and serviced by the PFLAG National Office, located in Washington, DC, the national Board of Directors and 13 Regional Directors. PFLAG promotes the health and well-being of lesbian, gay, bisexual and transgender persons, their families and friends through support, education and advocacy.
- Association des Parents Gays et Lesbiens (APGL)[13] is a French association founded in 1986 for those individuals or couples dealing with issues concerning their homosexuality and child-rearing and/or the desire to raise children. The APGL provides a supportive, non-judgemental space for the sharing and exchanging of experiences, reflections and ideas concerning parenting and the desire for children. The main goals of the association include: action for social and legal recognition of gay and lesbian families; help to end discrimination against gay men and lesbian women in the determination of their custody rights in divorce cases and in the processing of their applications to adopt as single persons; and equal rights, particularly those concerning adoption by same-sex couples, second parent adoption (when the child has a single known parent) and donor insemination for single lesbians or lesbian couples. APGL is also a place for debate and conviviality, where discussion groups, thematic debates, convivial weekends, evening events and activities for children are periodically organised.
- LGBTQ Parenting Connection[14] is a Canadian network of agencies, organisations and programmes whose primary focus is the support of lesbian, gay, bisexual, trans and **queer** parents, their children and their communities. Members of the LGBTQ Parenting Connection work to create healthy and informed communities within which LGBTQ families thrive. The LGBTQ Parenting Connection emerged as a collaboration between the original LGBT Parenting Network founded by the Family Service Association of Toronto (FSA) in 2001 (now Family Service Toronto; FST) and **queer** parenting programmes at The 519 Community Centre (The 519). With new

funding from the Ontario Ministry of Health and Long-Term Care in March 2006, the LGBT Parenting Network was moved from FSA to the Sherbourne Health Centre (SHC) in March 2007 and renamed the LGBTQ Parenting Network. Its main goals are: to enhance the health and well-being of LGBTQ-led families through local programmes and services; to provide knowledge, consultation and resources on LGBTQ-led families locally, provincially and beyond; to reduce social isolation and promote healthy, resilient LGBTQ-led families by providing information/support services to prospective parents, people at different stages of parenthood and their children; to promote culturally competent programmes and services for LGBTQ-led families and foster healthy, inclusive public policy through research, knowledge transfer, training and consultations with service providers and decision-makers; and to guide future programmes and services through evaluation and planning with input from clients, community members and service providers.

Notes

[1] See the Glossary at the end of the book for a presentation of the key concepts used in this chapter (highlighted in bold on first mention).

[2] There are 'female-to-male' (FtM) and 'male-to-female' (MtF) transitions. Female-to-male (FtM) people are born with female bodies or were identified as female at birth, but have a predominantly male gender identity, and people who were designated female at birth, but identify and live as male. Male-to-female (MtF) people are born with male bodies or were identified as male at birth, but have a predominantly female gender identity, and people who were designated male at birth, but identify and live as female.

[3] The DSM-IV is a manual published by the American Psychiatric Association that includes all currently recognised mental health disorders for both children and adults. It also lists known causes of these disorders, statistics in terms of gender, age at onset and prognosis, as well as some research concerning the 'optimal' treatment approaches (see: http://allpsych.com/disorders/dsm.html). (All websites cited in this chapter have been consulted in the period September–December 2012.)

[4] See: http://www.genderpsychology.org/transsexual/dsm_iv.html

[5] Homosexual couples cannot marry in Italy and they cannot adopt children or make use of assisted procreation. In particular, the current legislation on the issue of medically assisted procreation (MAP) is based on the highly

criticised and very restrictive Law 40 of 2004. This law forbids the use of MAP techniques of a heterologous type and forbids cryoconservation and the suppression of embryos. It also forbids the use of MAP techniques for single people, people below 18 years and people above fertile age. Only adult heterosexual couples, married or cohabiting, at a potentially fertile age, and where both partners are alive are allowed (*post mortem* fecundation is not permitted, ie, with the sperm of a partner who has died in the meantime). Thus, single men and women, widows, and homosexual couples are denied access to MAP. Because of all these heavy restrictions on the use and availability of assisted reproduction technologies, many Italians travel to other countries for fertility treatments (an increase of 200% since the introduction of Law 40).

[6] There are three different methods of artificial insemination, IUI, intracervical insemination (ICI) and intratubal insemination. Of these, IUI and ICI are the most common methods. The intratubal insemination method is comparatively rare due to its low success rates (see **Assisted reproductive technology (ART)** in the Glossary for details).

[7] See: http://www.insee.fr/fr/themes/document.asp?ref_id=ip1195

[8] For details on the National Survey on Family Growth–NSFG, see Chapter One, note 8 and: http://www.cdc.gov/nchs/nsfg.htm

[9] The AFCARS collects case-level information on all children in foster care for whom state child welfare agencies have responsibility for placement, care or supervision, and on children who are adopted under the auspices of the state's public child welfare agency (see: http://www.acf.hhs.gov/programs/cb/stats_research/).

[10] See: http://adoption.about.com/od/gaylesbian/f/gayparents.htm

[11] The majority of those with transsexual parents witnessed the transition. Altogether, 12 of the children were aware of their parent's sex change

[12] See: http://community.pflag.org/page.aspx?pid=237

[13] See: http://www.lgbtsupports.org/apgl/

[14] See: http://www.lgbtqparentingconnection.ca/home.cfm

References

Bailey, J.M., Bobrow, D., Wolfe, M. and Mikach, S. (1995) 'Sexual orientation of adult sons of gay fathers', *Developmental Psychology*, vol 31, no 1, pp 124–9.

Bertone, C. (2005) 'Esperienze di famiglia oltre l'eterosessualità' ['Family experiences beyond heterosexuality'], in E. Ruspini (ed) *Donne e uomini che cambiano. Relazioni di genere, identità sessuali e mutamento sociale*, Milano: Guerini, pp 239–61.

Bigner, J.J. and Jacobsen, R.B. (1989) 'Parenting behaviors of homosexual and heterosexual fathers', in F.W. Bozett (ed) *Homosexuality and the family*, New York, NY: Harrington Park Press, pp 173–86.

Bischof, G.H., Warnaar, B.L., Barajas, M.S. and Dhaliwal, H.K. (2011) 'Thematic analysis of the experiences of wives who stay with husbands who transition male-to-female', *Michigan Family Review*, vol 15, no 1, pp 16-34. Available at: http://quod.lib.umich.edu/m/mfr/4919087 .0015.102?rgn=main;view=fulltext

Bos, H.M.W., Van Balen, F. and Van Den Boom, D.C. (2004) 'Experience of parenthood, couple relationship, social support, and child-rearing goals in planned lesbian mother families', *Journal of Child Psychology and Psychiatry*, vol 45, pp 755–64.

Bottino, M. and Danna, D. (2005) *La gaia famiglia* [*The gay family*], Trieste: Asterios Editori.

Boyce, M. (2011) *When dad becomes mom:Exploring trans parenting*. Free e-book available at: http://www.fira.ca/cms/documents/168/ when_dad_becomes_mom.pdf

Bozett, F.W. (ed) (1987) *Gay and lesbian parents*, New York, NY: Praeger.

Bozett, F.W. (ed) (1989) *Homosexuality and the family*, New York, NY: The Haworth Press.

Bozett, F.W. and Sussman, M.B. (eds) (1990) *Homosexuality and family relations*, New York, NY: Harrington Park Press.

Buxton, A.P. (2009) 'Thoughts on a father's coming out to his children'. Available at: http://www.gayfathersboston.org/articles/amity.html

Epstein, R. and Duggan, S. (2006) 'Factors relating to parenting by non-heterosexual fathers', Father Involvement Community Research Forum, The Involvement Research Alliance CURA, Centre for Families, Work and Well-being, University of Guelph. Available at: http://www.fira.ca/cms/documents/44/Gay_Fathers.pdf

Fontaine, J.H. and Hammond, N.L. (1996) 'Counseling issues with gay and lesbian adolescents', *Adolescence*, vol 31, no 124, pp 817-30. Available at: http://www.questia.com/googleScholar.qst?docId=5000453831

Freedman, D., Tasker, F. and Di Ceglie, D. (2002) 'Children and adolescents with transsexual parents referred to a specialist gender identity development service: a brief report of key developmental features', *Clinical Child Psychology and Psychiatry*, vol 7, no 3, pp 423-32. Available at: http://www.acthe.fr/upload/Children_and_adolescents_with_transsexual_parents.pdf

Goldberg, A.E. and Allen, K.R. (2013) *LGBT-parent families. Innovations in research and implications for practice*, New York, NY: Springer.

Golombok, S., Spencer, A. and Rutter, M. (1983) 'Children in lesbian and single-parent households: psychosexual and psychiatric appraisal', *Journal of Child Psychology and Psychiatry*, vol 24, no 4, pp 551–72.

Gratton, E. (2008) *L'homoparentalité au masculin*, Paris: Presses Universitaires de France.

Green, R. (1978) 'Sexual identity of 37 children raised by homosexual or transsexual parents', *American Journal of Psychiatry*, vol 135, pp 692–7.

Green, R. (1998) 'Children of transsexual parents: research and clinical overview', in D. Di Ceglie and D. Freedman (eds) *A stranger in my own body: atypical gender identity development and mental health*, London: Karnac Books, pp 260–5.

Green, R., Mandel, J.B., Hotvedt, M.E., Gray, J. and Smith, L. (1986) 'Lesbian mothers and their children: a comparison with solo parent heterosexual mothers and their children', *Archives of Sexual Behavior*, vol 15, pp 167–84.

Gross, M. (2003) *L'homoparentalité*, Paris: Presses Universitaires de France.

Guidotto, N. (2005) 'Sharing scars, healing ourselves: theory in praxis', *Canadian Online Journal for Queer Studies in Education*, vol 3, no 1. Available at: http://jqstudies.library.utoronto.ca/index.php/jqstudies/article/view/3288/1422

Halberstam, J. (1998) *Female masculinity*, Durham, NC: Duke University Press.

Harris, M.B. and Turner, P.H. (1985/86) 'Gay and lesbian parents', *Journal of Homosexuality*, vol 12, no 2, pp 101–3.

Hines, S. (2006) 'Intimate transitions: transgender practices of partnering and parenting', *Sociology*, vol 40, no 2, pp 353–71.

Israel, G.E. (2004) 'Supporting transgender and sex reassignment issues: couple and family dynamics', in J.J. Bigner and J.L. Wetchler (eds) *Relationship therapy with same-sex couples*, New York, NY: Haworth Press, pp 53–63.

King, D. (1993) *The transvestite and the transsexual: public categories and private identities*, Aldershot: Avebury.

Lightfoot, M. (1998) 'Children of transsexual parents: issues facing the child of a transsexual parent', in D. Di Ceglie and D. Freedman (eds) *A stranger in my own body: atypical gender identity development and mental health*, London: Karnac Books, pp 275–85.

Luciani, S. (2010) 'Transizioni identitarie e transizioni familiari' ['Identity transitions and family transitions'], in E. Ruspini and S. Luciani (eds) *Nuovi genitori*, Roma: Carocci, pp 84–106.

Mallon, G.P. (2004) *Gay men choosing parenthood*, New York, NY: Columbia University Press.

Miller, J.A., Jacobsen, R.B. and Bigner, J.J. (1981) 'The child's home environment for lesbian–heterosexual mothers: a neglected area of research', *Journal of Homosexuality*, vol 7, no 1, pp 49–56.

Nadaud, S. (2002) *Homoparentalité: une nouvelle chance pour la famille?*, Paris: Fayard.

Patterson, C.J. (2004) 'Gay fathers', in M E. Lamb (ed) *The role of the father in child development* (4th edn), New York, NY: John Wiley and Sons, pp 397–416.

Patterson, C.J. (2005) 'Lesbian and gay parents and their children: summary of research findings', in American Psychological Association *Lesbian and Gay Parenting: A Resource for Psychologists* (2nd edn), Washington, DC: American Psychological Association.

Patterson, C.J. (2006) 'Children of lesbian and gay parents', *Current Directions in Psychological Science*, vol 15, no 5, pp 241–4. Available at: http://cdp.sagepub.com/content/15/5/241.full.pdf+html

Patterson, C.J. and Redding, R.E. (1996) 'Lesbian and gay families with children: implications of social science research for policy', *Journal of Social Issues*, vol 52, no 3, pp 29–50.

Pope, K.S., Tabachnick, B.G. and Keith-Spiegel, P. (1987) 'Ethics of practice: the beliefs and behaviors of psychologists as therapists', *American Psychologist*, vol 42, no 11, pp 993–1006.

Ray, V. and Gregory, R. (2001) 'School experiences of the children of lesbian and gay parents', *Family Matters*, no 59, Australian Institute of Family Studies. Available at: http://www.aifs.gov.au/institute/pubs/fm2001/fm59/vr.pdf

Ruspini, E. (2010a) 'Madri, padri, figli, omosessualità' ['Mothers, fathers, children, homosexuality'], in E. Ruspini and S. Luciani (eds) *Nuovi genitori*, Roma: Carocci, pp 64–83.

Ruspini, E. (2010b) 'Italian homosexual fathers between stereotypes and desire for paternity', Symposium 'LGBT parenting: a resource and a challenge for social policy' (organised by Elisabetta Ruspini and Sally Hines), Social Policy Association Annual Conference, University of Lincoln, 5–7 July.

Sales, J. (1995) 'Children of a transsexual father: a successful intervention', *European Child & Adolescent Psychiatry*, vol 4, pp 136–9.

Scallen, R.M. (1982) 'An investigation of parental attitudes and behaviors in homosexual and heterosexual fathers', *Dissertation Abstract International*, vol 42 (9-B).

Segal-Engelchin, D., Erera, P.I and Cwikel, C. (2005) 'The hetero-gay family: an emergent family configuration', *Journal of GLBT Family Studies*, vol 1, no 3, pp 85–104.

Shanley, M.L. (2002) *Making babies, making families. What matters most in an age of reproductive technologies, surrogacy, adoption, and same-sex and unwed parents*, Boston, MA: Beacon Press.

Stacey, J. (2002) 'Gay and lesbian families are here; all our families are queer; let's get used to it!', in C.L. Williams and A. Stein (eds) *Sexuality and gender*, Oxford: Blackwell, pp 395–407.

Stacey, J. and Biblarz, T.J. (2001) '(How) Does the sexual orientation of parents matter?', *American Sociological Review*, vol 66, no 2, pp 159–83.

Sullivan, N. (2003) *A critical introduction to queer theory*, New York: New York University Press.

Tasker, F.L. and Golombok, S. (1997) *Growing up in a lesbian family. Effects on child development*, New York, NY: The Guilford Press.

Tully, B. (1992) *Accounting for transsexualism and transhomosexuality*, London: Whiting & Birch.

White, T. and Ettner, R. (2004) 'Disclosure, risks and protective factors for children whose parents are undergoing a gender transition', *Journal of Gay & Lesbian Psychotherapy*, vol 8, nos 1/2, pp 129–45.

CONCLUSIONS

What can we learn?

The aim of this book has been to show that it is now becoming possible to live, love and form a family without sex, without children, without a shared home, without a (male or female) partner, without a working husband, without a heterosexual orientation and without a 'biological' sexual body. As we have seen, the presence of the Millennial generation and the Web 2.0 culture and environment greatly helps.

The force of the Millennials, the positive qualities of young people who have grown up in a globalised, changing and reflexive world, has overturned many commonplaces and stereotypes (Greenberg and Weber, 2008; Taylor and Keeter, 2010; Rainer and Rainer, 2011; Stanton and Hess, 2012). Millennials are more accepting than were older generations of non-traditional family arrangements, from mothers of young children working outside the home, to adults living together without being married. And the Millennials are also distinctive in their social values; they stand out in their acceptance of homosexuality, interracial dating and expanded roles for women and immigrants (Taylor and Keeter, 2010).

The main question that has motivated much of the thinking behind this book is the following: are changing gender identities and roles influencing planning choices among couples, the processes of family formation and models of fatherhood and motherhood, and, if so, how and in what ways? We have also tried to describe how the changes in relationships and family life fit into the bigger pattern of cultural change in the last few decades, trying to understand the reciprocal interconnection between the cultures of the past and contemporary generations. The interplay between past and present raises the crucial question of how the 'new' digital and Millennial modernity relates to and interacts with the 'old': how institutions, norms, rules and structures of modernity coexist and interpenetrate the new.

Conceptualising contemporary modernity (see, eg, Lyotard, 1979; Giddens, 1990, 1991; Bauman, 1992; Beck, 1992; Beck and Beck-Gernsheim, 2001; Taylor-Gooby, 2005; Beck and Grande, 2010), it becomes more and more crucial to consider the interplay, tensions and contradictions between modernity's 'imperative of stability and order', including the expression of collective identities and interests, and the fragmentation, individualisation and fluidity of contemporary (gender) identities.

In contemporary modernity, men and women have many more possibilities to shape their own destinies, and, at the same time, individual striving for fulfilment has challenged traditional family norms. Over the past 40 years, there have been changes in social norms and attitudes with respect to partnership, family formation and parenthood. The nuclear family consisting of a father, mother and their child or children is declining; divorce and cohabitation rates are increasing rapidly, and women and men are having their children at a much later age and having fewer children than ever before. At the same time, the number of lone mothers and lone fathers is increasing; more adults than ever before are living alone or with unmarried partners, and the numbers of childfree couples are growing. This has exerted a significant effect on family planning and family life. As a result, there are more choices and possibilities for negotiating available lifestyles. Within this complex and evolving scenario, one of the most striking changes in family composition has been the escalating number of lone-parent families, with a prevalence of lone mothers over lone fathers. The childfree attitude is also growing: more and more women, men and couples are choosing not to procreate. The phenomenon of living apart together (LAT) couples may also be seen as one of the most important manifestations of the 'personalisation' and 'flexibilisation' of relationships in contemporary modernity. Asexual relationships also allow us to understand how people can negotiate the social pressures around sex and sexuality in relationships. Moreover, they offer the possibility to reflect upon gender relationships independent of the sexual dimension.

Another area in which **gender roles**[1] have changed the most involves men's roles (see, eg, Pease and Pringle, 2001; Ruspini et al, 2011). For example, men are beginning to claim a greater share in bringing up their children: they are, in general, spending more time with their children (changing diapers, playing), albeit still at a lower level than mothers (Coltrane, 1996; Doucet, 2006). The desire to discover (or rediscover) the terms and values of their specific masculinity also seems to be growing. This leads to explicit breaks with traditional forms of masculinity. Following Hooks (2004), challenging patriarchy is a very necessary element for men's and women's liberation (Pease, 2000).

Finally, these living arrangements question the traditional model of the organisation of family life and radically challenge many **gender stereotypes** (Basow, 1992; Lorber, 1994). There also seems to be a growing space for a more egalitarian division of sex roles and a rejection of traditional patriarchal arrangements in contemporary families.

Thus, comparisons of late- or post-modern families to other family configurations help highlight central issues and offer directions for future research and social policy development. 'Traditional' institutional approaches to citizenship are often obsolete, weak or absent in the face of the demands of complex, multicultural and reflexive individuals, families and societies. In consequence, theorisations of late or post-modernity might improve understanding of welfare issues and needs (see, eg, Leonard, 1997; Carter, 1998).

Comparison of traditional and modern approaches also helps the planning and implementation of educational schemes. For example, such efforts might help children and adolescents approach and understand family change, asexuality, homosexuality and **transsexuality** and, more importantly, help the children of asexuals, lone mothers and fathers, LAT couples, stay-at-home fathers, and homosexual and transsexual families. Asexual, LAT, lone, homosexual and trans parenting are not only 'risk factors' for children's development, they also represent opportunities to multiply the affective dynamics between family members that will aid in reducing gender stereotypes. As DePaulo wrote:

> There are so many ways to live and love. The sentimentalized image of mom, dad and the kids gathered around the hearth has had its day.... We're not all going nuclear anymore.... When people organically develop their own experiments in living, the results can be far more fulfilling than the solutions unpacked from the same old boxes from the past.[2]

Social research must take into account and explore all these novelties. This means not only documenting already-known phenomena. Indeed, a broadening in the following directions has become a necessity:

- First, we need to have a better understanding of the tension between **socialisation** processes and **gender identity, gender stereotypes** and ongoing trends in **social change**. While, on the one hand, these trends seem to lead towards a flattening of gender differences and to a convergence of **life courses**, on the other hand, socialisation agencies are still unable to guarantee adequate training for the needs arising from recent changes in female and male identities. It is also increasingly necessary to understand and work through the consequent tensions and changes that have affected the social organisation of gender relations in order to work towards a deconstruction of the discriminatory socialisation that affects not only girls (who are trained for caring tasks, secondary social roles and renouncement), but also boys (in supporting the rigidity of the dominant male model and rejecting any adaptation to ongoing processes of social change).

- Second, we need more studies that explore the evolving connections among the social construction of gender identities, the plurality of sexual orientations and strategies of family formation that affect contemporary forms of cohabitation, motherhood and fatherhood. This shift in family forms should be regarded as a requirement for the intervention of the welfare state in its efforts to reconcile work and family obligations (for both genders).

- Third, the field of masculinity studies needs further development. While changes in the roles of women have been widely debated in the last 10 years and resulted in changes in both women's and men's ideas and practices, those relating to men have been much less discussed. Are men adapting to the changing gender environment? How might we (women and men, families, institutions, society) support this process of adaptation and men's commitments to care? Our opinion is that there cannot be gender equality without the participation of men; that is, without a change (and a social acceptance of this change) in the ways of feeling and thinking of men themselves.

- Fourth, we urgently need to gain a better understanding of the relationship between family diversity and advanced internet technologies (see, eg, Pauwels, 2006; Richter, 2010). How do websites, blogs, forums and so on present the family? How do they talk about family diversity? Can social computing strategies empower under-represented and misrepresented groups? Digital access and capabilities in dealing with ICT have been identified as relevant for personal fulfilment and development, active citizenship, social inclusion and employment (Warschauer, 2003). New media technologies for social networking such as Facebook, MySpace, Twitter and YouTube, are transforming the social, political, informational, relational, and affective practices of individuals and institutions. The Web 2.0 platform includes devices such as blogs, wikis, podcasting, and vodcasting that can be mobilised for global citizenship (Cifuentes et al, 2011). Web 2.0 can facilitate communication, information gathering and sharing, interoperability, user-centered design, and collaboration (Hofstede, 1997). Web 2.0 technologies also offer social support, that is, the degree to which a person's basic social needs are gratified through interaction with others (Ridings and Gefen, 2004). Web 2.0 may thus promote friendship, solidarity, and active citizenship.

As a final consideration, we may say that a more balanced and more attentive vision of the ongoing processes of individual and family change seems fundamental to resolve many of the problems that today affect relations between genders and generations.

Notes

[1] See the Glossary at the end of the book for a presentation of the key concepts used in this chapter (highlighted in bold on first mention).

[2] From: http://www.nytimes.com/roomfordebate/2012/02/12/the-advantages-and-disadvantages-of-living-alone/living-apart-and-together-the-optimum-balance (all websites cited in this chapter have been consulted in the period September–December 2012).

References

Basow, S.A. (1992) *Gender: stereotypes and roles* (3rd edn), Pacific Grove, CA: Thomson Learning.

Bauman, Z. (1992) *Intimations of postmodernity*, New York, NY, and London: Routledge.

Beck, U. (1992) *Risk society: towards a new modernity*, London: Sage Publications.

Beck, U. and Beck-Gernsheim, E. (2001) *Individualization. Institutionalized individualism and its social and political consequences*, London: Sage Publications.

Beck, U. and Grande, E. (2010) 'Varieties of second modernity: the cosmopolitan turn in social and political theory and research', *British Journal of Sociology*, vol 61, no 3, pp 409–43.

Carter, J. (ed) (1998) *Postmodernity and the fragmentation of welfare*, London: Routledge.

Cifuentes, L., Merchant, Z. and Vural, Ö.F. (2011) 'Web 2.0 technologies forge the way for global citizenship', *Mustafa Kemal University Journal of Social Sciences Institute*, vol 8, no 15, pp 295–312. Available at: http://old.mku.edu.tr/image/sosyalbilimleri/file/sayi_onbes/15_Cifuentes_Merchant_Vural.pdf

Coltrane, S. (1996) *Family man: fatherhood, housework, and gender equity*, Oxford: Oxford University Press.

Doucet, A. (2006) *Do men mother? Fathering, care, and domestic responsibility*, Toronto: University of Toronto Press.

Giddens, A. (1990) *The consequences of modernity*, Cambridge: Polity Press.

Giddens, A. (1991) *Modernity and self-identity. Self and society in the late modern age*, Cambridge: Polity Press.

Greenberg, E.H. and Weber, K. (2008) *Generation we: how Millennial youth are taking over America and changing our world forever*, Pachatusan.

Hofstede, G. (1997) *Cultures and organizations, software of the mind: intercultural cooperation and its importance for survival*, New York, NY: McGraw-Hill.

Hooks, B. (2004) *The will to change: men, masculinity and love*, Washington Square Press.

Leonard, P. (1997) *Postmodern welfare: reconstructing an emancipatory project*, London: Sage Publications.

Lorber, J. (1994) *Paradoxes of gender*, New Haven, CT, and London: Yale University Press.

Lyotard, J.-F. (1979) *La condition postmoderne: rapport sur le savoir*, Paris: Minuit (English translation: Lyotard, J.-F. [1984] *The postmodern condition: a report on knowledge*, Manchester: Manchester University Press).

Pauwels, L. (2006) 'On the visual, verbal and graphic construal and decoding of cultural values in cyberspace', in R. Griffin, B. Doyle Cowden and M. Avgerinou (eds) *Imagery and artistry, animating the mind's eye*, Loretto, PA: International Visual Literacy Association, pp 153–8.

Pease, B. (2000) *Recreating men: postmodern masculinity politics*, London: Sage.

Pease, B. and Pringle, K. (eds) (2001) *A man's world? Changing men's practices in a globalized world*, London: Zed Books.

Rainer, T. and Rainer, J. (2011) *The Millennials: connecting to America's largest generation*, Nashville: B&H Publishing Group.

Richter, R. (2010) Images of the family. How to define them through sociological-empirical data', in O. Kapella, C. Rille-Pfeiffer, M. Rupp and N.F. Schneider (eds) *Family diversity: collection of the 3rd European Congress of Family Science*, Berlin: Barbara Budrich Publishers, pp 85–94.

Ridings, C.M. and Gefen, D. (2004) 'Virtual community attraction: why people hand out online', *Journal of Computer-Mediated Communication*, vol 10, no 1, http://jcmc.indiana.edu/vol10/issue1/ridings_gefen.html

Ruspini, E., Hearn, J., Pease, B. and Pringle, K. (eds) (2011) *Men and masculinities around the world. Transforming men's practices*, Global Masculinities Series, Basingstoke: Palgrave Macmillan.

Stanton, G.T. and Hess, A. (2012) 'Generational values and desires', Focus on the Family Findings. Available at: http://www.focusonthefamily.com/about_us/focus-findings/family-formation-trends/generational-values-desires.aspx

Taylor, P. and Keeter, S. (eds) (2010) *Millennials: a portrait of generation next. Confident, connected, open to change,* Washington, DC: Pew Research Center. Available at: http://www.pewsocialtrends.org/files/2010/10/millennials-confident-connected-open-to-change.pdf

Taylor-Gooby, P. (2005) 'Pervasive uncertainty in second modernity: an empirical test', *Sociological Research Online,* vol 10, issue 4. Available at: http://www.socresonline.org.uk/10/4/taylor-gooby.html

Warschauer, M. (2003) *Technology and social inclusion: Rethinking the digital divide,* Cambridge: MIT Press.

Glossary of key concepts

Assisted reproductive technology (ART) is a term referring to methods used to achieve pregnancy by artificial or partially artificial means. Reproductive technologies include:[1]

- collecting and storing sperm or eggs (below 0°C) for artificial insemination;
- artificial insemination, in which collected sperm are placed in the reproductive system of a woman;
- in vitro fertilisation (IVF), in which collected sperm and eggs are placed in a test tube for fertilisation, and the developing egg is then placed in the reproductive system of a woman; and
- storage of developing fertilised eggs (embryos) for later use if an initial implantation of fertilised eggs produced by the IVF procedure fails.

Baby Boom refers to a period of increased birth rates lasting from 1946 to the mid-1960s. There is some disagreement as to the precise beginning and ending dates of the post-war baby boom, but it is most often agreed that it began in the years immediately after the war, ending more than a decade later.

Baby Boomers are men and women born between 1946 and 1964, and are now predominantly in their 50s and 60s. Early Baby Boomers were born 1946–54; late Baby Boomers between 1956 and 1964. Early Baby Boomers are generally optimistic and they think themselves as a special generation that changed the world, so much so that they created their own lifestyle by bringing new changes to society. Even if Baby Boomers are associated with a rejection or redefinition of traditional values, many commentators have disputed the extent of that rejection, noting the widespread continuity of values with older and younger generations. Baby Boomers are today well-established in their careers and hold positions of power and authority (Howe and Strauss, 1991). Late Boomers are much more vulnerable: they did not benefit as much from the main bull market (1982–2000) as did the early Boomers, and they were hit just as hard in the recent financial crisis.

Coming out is the process of recognition, acknowledgement and revelation of one's sexual orientation and gender identity. Experiences of coming out may be very different. There are many diverse variables that relate to coming out, including: family, culture, race, ethnicity, religion, gender, age, political affiliation or being differently-abled (see, eg, Davies, 1992; Hunter, 2007).

Commuting (or commuter) marriages have been defined as voluntary arrangements where dual-career couples maintain two residences in different geographic locations and are separated at least three nights per week for a minimum of three months (Gerstel and Gross, 1982; Orton and Crossman, 1988); that is, unions in which partners live apart for reasons other than a legal separation (usually because of the locations of their jobs) and who regularly travel to be together, as on weekends. These living arrangements are multiplying. According to an analysis of Census figures by the Center for the Study of Long-Distance Relationships, their number jumped 30% to 3.6 million in the US from 2000 to 2005. It is harder to know precisely how many non-married couples are in a long-distance relationship, but according to the Center for the Study of Long-Distance Relationships, there were an estimated 4–4.5 million college couples in the US in non-marital long-distance relationships.[2]

Culture refers to all the symbols, beliefs, meanings, behaviours, values and objects shared by members of a particular group, in contrast to other groups. People and groups define themselves, understand meanings, derive social expectations and conform to society's shared values through culture. Culture is a key concept in sociology. Themes such as religious beliefs, norms and values, the motivations for individual actions, and socialisation processes have been at the heart of sociological investigations of human life, both in the period of the classical sociologists and throughout the 20th century (eg Emile Durkheim, Karl Marx, Georg Simmel, Max Weber, the Frankfurt School, Harold Garfinkel, Erving Goffman, Pierre Bourdieu, etc). Cultural sociologists treat as culture all socially located forms and processes of human meaning-making, whether or not they occur in specialised institutions, and whether or not they are confined to one clearly bounded group. Cultural sociologists investigate how meaning-making happens, why meanings and values vary, how values and meanings influence human action, and the ways that meaning-making generates solidarity and conflict (Spillman, 2002).

Gender refers to the socially constructed roles, behaviours, desires, activities and attributes that a given society considers appropriate for men and women. In other words, it is the social construction of female and male bodies. Gender is often misunderstood as referring only to women. However, the concept refers both to men and women, the relationship and division of labour between them, their roles, their access to and control over resources, and their interests and needs (Woodward, 2011). Conversely, *sex*, assigned at birth, refers to one's biological status as either male or female, and is associated primarily with physical and physiological attributes such as chromosomes, hormone prevalence and external and internal anatomy. Embryos are identical, regardless of genetic sex, until a certain point in development (sixth week of pregnancy), then the indifferent gonads begin to differentiate according to genetic sex. It is the Testis-Determining Factor (TDF) that causes male sex organs to develop, whereas the lack of this factor will cause the embryo to develop as physically female. Following Judith Lorber (2001), biological sex is not binary (to male and female), you can add hermaphrodite and transsexual. Physiologically, there is overlap in muscular strength and physical endurance – a continuum rather than a male–female split.[3]

Gender identity may be defined as the personal conception of oneself as a man or woman (or as both or neither, ie, the refusal to label oneself). For example, if a person considers himself a male and is most comfortable referring to his personal gender in masculine terms, then his gender identity is male. The process of gender acquisition may be fully, somewhat or not at all concordant with biological sex or with social expectations related to it. Gender identity does not cause sexual orientation. For example, a 'masculine' woman is not necessarily a lesbian. Gender identity is fundamentally different from a person's sexual orientation (Woodward, 2011).

Gender relations are the ways in which a culture or society defines the desires, rights, responsibilities and identities of men and women in relation to one another. The term refers to the set of social, behavioural and sexual norms that are considered socially 'appropriate' for the interaction between women and men in the context of a specific culture (Woodward, 2011).

Gender roles refer to the set of social, behavioural, and sexual norms that are considered socially 'appropriate' for women and men in the context of a specific culture. Each society assigns different people roles according to their gender. For example, women are supposed to be modest, tender, intuitive, submissive and concerned with care issues in a number of cultures. Many cultures expect men to work for pay outside the home, be rational, dominant and aggressive (Kimmel, 1996). Gender roles differ widely between cultures, classes, ages, generations, and across historical periods (Woodward, 2011).

Gender stereotypes are simplistic generalisations about the gender attributes, differences and roles of individuals and/or groups. Stereotypes can be positive or negative, but they rarely communicate accurate information about others. When people automatically apply gender assumptions to others regardless of evidence to the contrary, they are perpetuating gender stereotyping (Basow, 1992). Common and widely held gender stereotypes include the following: 'Men are naturally attracted to women; women are naturally attracted to men'; 'A marriage without sex is not even really a marriage'; 'All capable couples should have children'; 'If you are male, then you must be sexual'; 'Having children is good'; 'A couple's (woman's; man's) life cannot possibly be complete without children'; 'Couples (women; men) with children are happier than childfree couples'; 'Children must stay with their mother'; 'Women are made to be wives and mothers'; 'Women are fulfilled when they become mothers, and men in supporting their family'; 'Fathers are not suited to caring activities'; 'Gays and lesbians are unable to have lasting relationships; they represent sexual excess'; 'Gays and lesbians cannot take care of children; they are a threat for "real" families'; 'Homosexuality and bisexuality represent a confusion between the sexes'; and 'Transsexuals suffer from serious mental disorders'.

Generation X, a term popularised by Douglas Coupland's (1991) novel *Generation X: Tales for an accelerated culture* concerning young adults during the late 1980s and their lifestyles, is a term used to describe the generation born after the Baby Boom ended. Most demographers agree that Generation Xers were born between 1964 and 1984. This generation is often referred to as Baby Busters, as they are attributed to a rapid decline in birth rates after the Baby Boomers. Generation X is thus used to describe a generational change from the later Baby Boomer cohort who were born in the late 1950s.

Homo-parenthood is a neologism, created in 1997 by the French Association of Gay and Lesbian Parents (Association des Parents Gays et Lesbiens; APGL),[4] denoting a situation in which at least one adult refers to him or herself as homosexual who is or wishes to be a father or mother of at least one child (Gross, 2003). The term 'homo-parenthood' may also be defined as a political strategy to give visibility to gays, lesbians and transsexuals who are or wish to become fathers and mothers (Uziel, Silva da Cunha and Torres, 2007).

Identity is defined as people's source of meaning and experience (Berger and Luckmann, 1967). Identity is a relational concept: the formation of one's identity occurs through one's identifications with significant others (primarily with parents) and other individuals during one's life course, and also with groups. Social identity may be defined as one's sense of self as a member of a social group (or groups).

Independence is a fluid and multi-dimensional concept (Land, 1986, 1989; Lister 1990), thus difficult to define and measure. This because the concept of dependency is very complex. There are, indeed, several types of dependency. Fraser and Gordon (1994) talk about a semantic geography of dependencies. Dependency can be expressed in economic terms, for example a person may depend on another or on an institution for her/his subsistence. Dependency can also be expressed sociolegally, politically or psychologically. Dependency can manifest itself in different fields, such as the private sphere (women dependent on their partner or the family network) and the public sphere (women dependent on social policies). Dependency is socially and institutionally constructed: we may, for example, think of the assumption that men maintain the right to appropriate female time for housework, caring and maintenance; that children 'need their mothers'; that women are 'better carers'; that women are dependent on the male/family income; that dependence on welfare provision is 'bad' and therefore stigmatised, while private forms of dependency are legitimised and socially accepted. Independence may be reached through education, employment and/or public childcare. Independence should also be understood as the possibility to make choices free from emotional and psychological dependence. One key dimension of independence is the economic one. According to the Federal/Provincial/Territorial Status of Women Ministers (2001), economic independence may be defined as a condition where individual women and men have full access to the range of economic opportunities and resources, including employment, services and sufficient disposable income, in order that they can shape their lives and meet their own needs and those of their dependants. Other terms that have been used to describe the concept of independence are 'autonomy' or 'self-sufficiency' (see also Land, 1986, 1989).

Intimacy refers to a strong physical, emotional, mental, spiritual and/
or social closeness or connection. Intimate relationships may or may
not include sexual intimacy.

Life course refers to the history of each family or individual and to
the way this history evolves and changes over time. The life course is
determined by interdependent trajectories and transitions that subjects
(individual or collective; woman, man, couple, firm) undergo during
the course of their existence. Trajectories refer to the path taken as
time goes on within a specific and relatively long-term experience of
or position in the family, work and so on, one that may often continue
for a large part of the individual's lifespan. Transitions reflect the
fluctuations/changes within a trajectory: in other words, trajectories
are characterised by the transitions, or changes, of social, economic
and demographic interests that evolve in response to specific events
(Elder, 1985, 1992). In this instance, 'event' is taken to mean a change,
or a transition, from one discrete state to another, a passage that takes
place at a specific point in time and that constitutes a radical departure
from what came before the 'catalysing' event: for example, marriage,
the birth of a child, starting work, divorce and so on (Allison, 1984).
Thus, an event can be defined as a change that gives an individual a
new status that is different from the previous status the individual was
in before the change took place.

Longitudinal is a broad term. Longitudinal data can be defined as data
on a number of variables gathered during the observation of subjects
over time. This definition implies the notion of repeated measurements
(van der Kamp and Bijleveld, 1998). Basically, longitudinal data present
information about what happened to a set of units (people, households,
firms, etc) across time. The participants in a typical longitudinal study
are asked to provide information about their behaviour and attitudes
regarding the issues of interest on a number of separate occasions in
time (called the 'waves' of the study) (see, eg, Taris, 2000). In contrast,
cross-sectional data refer to the circumstances of respondents at one
particular point in time. Thus, the term longitudinal refers to a particular
type of relation between phenomena: the type that evolves over the
course of time, which is termed *diachronic*, the opposite of *synchronic*
(Ruspini, 2002).

Queer has been defined as a political statement, as well as a sexual
orientation, which advocates breaking binary thinking and seeing
both sexual orientation and gender identity as potentially fluid (Kirsch,

2000). Queer theory attacks the gender order directly by multiplying gender categories and undermining the boundaries between women and men, female and male. In Queer theory, gender and sexuality are 'performances' – identities or selves we create as we act and interact with others (Lorber, 2000, 2010). Queer theory also challenges the notions of homosexuality and heterosexuality, and instead posits an understanding of sexuality that emphasises shifting boundaries, ambivalences and cultural constructions that change depending on historical and cultural context.[6]

Secondary analysis involves the use of existing data, collected for the purposes of a prior study, in order to pursue a research interest which is distinct from that of the original work; this may be a new research question or an alternative perspective on the original question (Heaton, 1998; Smith, 2006; Boslaugh, 2007). An analysis of secondary data thus describes a research approach in which existing data are re-analysed. Secondary analysis can involve the use of single or multiple qualitative data sets, as well as mixed qualitative and quantitative data sets. In addition, the approach may either be employed by researchers to re-use their own data or by independent analysts using previously established qualitative data sets. This includes census data, the website of the agency or other entity responsible for collecting and/or making the data available, published reports, research articles based on the data, and personal communications with relevant individuals, newspapers, and so on. Secondary data can be a valuable source of information for gaining knowledge and insight into a broad range of issues and phenomena.

Second-wave feminism differentiates the women's movement that began in the late 1960s from the suffrage movement of the late 19th and early 20th centuries (or 'first-wave' feminism). First-wave feminism arose in the context of industrial society and liberal politics but was connected to both the progressive women's rights movement and early socialist feminism in the late 19th and early 20th century in the US and Europe. The key concerns of first-wave feminists were education, the right to vote (women's suffrage) and equal opportunities for women. The term 'second wave' refers to the increase in feminist activity that occurred in the US, Britain and Europe from the late 1960s until the end of the 1970s as an offshoot of the civil rights and anti-war movements. Second-wave feminists sought to achieve equality for women by challenging unfair labour practices and discriminatory laws. They provided women with educational material about sex and reproduction and fought to legalise all forms of birth control. They established political organisations and wrote books, articles and essays challenging sexism in society. Third-wave feminism began in the late 1980s as a response to the perceived failures of the second wave. It is a theoretical perspective that is both a continuation of and a break with second-wave feminism. It shared many of the interests of the first two waves, that is, the empowerment of women, but it is also attributed to the desire of women to find a voice of their own and to include various diverse groups like women of colour and lesbian, bisexual and trans women. It builds on multi-racial/multi-ethnic feminism, feminist studies of men and postmodern feminism (Lorber, 2000, 2010). Fourth-wave feminism started after the beginning of the 21st century. As Erbe (2012) writes, this wave is, or will be, a child of the internet. Websites such as Jezebel (see: http://jezebel.com/feminism/) and Feministing (see: http://feministing.com/) have allowed young women to raise issues and express opinions (and to organise) in a way that print publications never afforded (Erbe, 2012). Fourth-wave feminism (or 'first-wave equalism') has been defined as follows:[4]

> It is about: 1) Fighting sexism (on all counts), which should include fighting the social oppression that men have suffered over the years (i.e., with the way they dress, they have to be macho, boys don't cry/wear make-up/wear pink/wear a skirt). This should also include reverse sexism – female's sexism toward males – which seems to be prevalent in some of 'feminist's' blogs. 2) Fighting internalized misogyny. 3) Fighting against the social norm to make jokes about 'Women belonging in the kitchen' or 'Putting women in "their place"'. Jokes like this fuel sexism and make us desensitized. 4) Fighting against spousal abuse/domestic violence/all forms of assaults and harassment, regardless of gender. 5) Fighting against all forms of gender oppression. 6) Fighting homophobia and heterosexism, and prejudice toward transgender people and non-gendered people – but also making sure no one discriminates against cisgendered,[5] straight people in the process, which has been seen and experienced. 7) Fighting species-ism. That Cow is no different than that Dog. 8) Fighting racism, internalized racism and all kinds of race-discrimination (this includes White on Black, Black on White, Asian on Black, Asian on Hispanic, Hispanic on Asian etc. etc.).

Sexuality is how people experience and express themselves as sexual beings. The concept of what activities, desires, feelings and sensations are 'sexual' is historically and culturally determined. Sexual meanings are social and cultural constructs, they are made subjective only after cultural and social mediation (Foucault, 1976–84). Sexuality varies from culture to culture, changes within a culture over time and changes over the course of each of our lives. Sexuality is not only the biological datum (being sexed and having sexual relations), but a relational aspect of the individual identity (Giddens, 1992). Following Lorber (2001), sexuality is not binary or fixed. There are at least six sexualities: heterosexual woman, heterosexual man, lesbian, gay man, bisexual man and bisexual woman. These gendered sexual statuses encompass a variety of feelings and experiences.

Sexual orientation describes a person's romantic, emotional or sexual attraction to another person. It is the 'direction' of one's sexuality and sexual interest: to the opposite sex (heterosexual), the same sex (homosexual), both (bisexual) or neither (asexual). The concept of sexual orientation refers to more than sexual behaviour. It includes feelings as well as identity. Sexual orientation is not innate and fixed, however; sexual orientation develops across a person's lifetime. Individuals may become aware at different points in their lives that they are heterosexual, gay, lesbian, bisexual or asexual.

Social change, in Sociology, refers to a major change in a society or culture that has lasting effects on that culture. Social change may include changes in nature, social institutions, social behaviours or social relations. The modern social sciences have emerged as a response to an era of very rapid, all-embracing social changes – namely, the development of capitalism, which radically changed the older forms of social organisation, most notably, of the feudal system – and to the consequent need for greater understanding of social, cultural, economic and political processes. Social change played a central role in classical sociological thought. Auguste Comte considered historical comparison to be the tool on which sociological research was based. Sociology is nothing if it is not guided by knowledge of historical evolution:

> historical comparison of the diverse consecutive states of humanity is not only the main scientific insight of the new political philosophy … it also directly forms the basis of the science, of what it can offer as being most typical. (Comte, 1842, p 268)

The notion of differentiation (or specialisation) was central in the work of Herbert Spencer, Emile Durkheim and Talcott Parsons. Karl Marx described the dynamics of the capitalist system. Capitalist development is achieved though expropriation of surplus value, or profit, by the capitalist, from the workers. Indeed, Marx posited contradictions and conflicts as arising from the differentiation of economic and social positions in economic systems. Max Weber established the dynamic power of culture, particularly religion, in social change (Smelser, 1981; Haferkamp and Smelser, 1992). Furthermore, Abrams (1982) argued that sociological explanations must always be of a historical nature, because social reality is a historical reality, a reality in time, while, according to Wright Mills (1959), social science deals with the problems of biography, history and of the way they affect the body of social structures.

Socialisation is the process of learning how to behave in ways that are understandable and acceptable to social expectations. Through socialisation, the values, norms and practical know-how of a society are handed down from generation to generation. Through socialisation individuals are made aware of behaviours that are expected of them with regard to the norms, beliefs, attitudes and values of the society in which they live. As a process, it begins at birth and continues throughout our lifespan. There are several agencies of socialisation: family; school system; peer groups; media; religion; work environment; and volunteer groups. These agencies are responsible for the processes through which individuals learn 'appropriate' behaviours as members of a smaller group within the larger society. Generally, contemporary agencies of socialisation (with notably rare exceptions) support fertility and negatively judge a woman or a man that does not want to have children (see, eg, Grusek and Hastings, 2007).

Social reproduction refers to processes that perpetuate characteristics of social structure over periods of time. It entails 'the biological reproduction of the labour force, both generationally and on a daily basis, including the provision of "food, shelter, clothing, and health care"' (Katz, 2001, p 710). Social reproduction thus includes the care and socialisation of children and the care of the elderly or infirm. These processes are both historically and culturally contingent.

Surrogate motherhood may be defined as an agreement between a person or couple who wish to raise a child and a woman who is willing to carry and deliver the child. This woman, the surrogate mother, may be the child's genetic mother, or she may be genetically unrelated to the child. The surrogate mother may receive compensation beyond the reimbursement of medical and other reasonable expenses. A surrogate pregnancy is different from adoption in that the woman who will carry and give birth to the child is not pregnant at the time the surrogacy arrangements are made. There are a variety of ways in which the surrogate mother can become pregnant, as well as a variety of reasons why prospective mothers and fathers choose this approach to reproduction.[8]

Transgender is an umbrella term (ie a single common category that covers multiple terms) referring to anyone who crosses traditional gender norms for a man or woman in society (Monro, 2006). It refers to people who are not comfortable with or who reject, in whole or in part, their birth-assigned gender identities. It includes transsexuals, cross-dressers and intersexed individuals. The personal characteristics that are associated with gender identity include self-image, physical and biological appearance, and behaviour and conduct, as they relate to gender. Gender identity is fundamentally different from a person's sexual orientation.[9] Some transgendered individuals try to surgically modify their body to fit the physical form that they feel is appropriate, while others do not. If they do not want surgical intervention, they may make the kinds of alterations to their physical appearance that allow them to conform as closely as possible to the gender they feel is correct for them.

Transsexuality is the experience of a discrepancy between genetic or assigned (anatomical) sex and sexual identity. Often, transsexual people alter or wish to alter their bodies through hormones or surgery in order to make it match their gender identity. Transsexuality may thus be defined as a phase, or passage, from one sex to another – a transition to the 'opposite' sex. The 'ultimate' outcome of this process is surgical intervention, a reconstruction of the body that aims at creating harmony between an individual's sexual identity and her/his body. In this way, a person who is genetically male – that is, who has been identified as sexually male – may transition to female (male-to-female [MtF]) and vice versa (female-to-male [FtM]) (Garfinkel, 1967; Prosser, 1998).

Notes

[1] See: http://education.technyou.edu.au/view/246/reproductive-technologies (all websites cited in the Glossary have been consulted in the period September–December 2012).

[2] See: http://www.waiit.com/Long_Distance_Relationships_Statistics

[3] See: http://www.lgbtsupports.org/apgl/

[4] From: http://www.tumblr.com/tagged/fourth%20wave%20feminism

[5] In gender studies, 'cisgender' defines individuals who have a match between the gender they were assigned at birth, their bodies and their personal identity. A similar adjective is 'gender-normative'. Cisgendered is, as such, a complementary designation to the term transgendered.

[6] See: http://geneq.berkeley.edu/lgbt_resources_definiton_of_terms and http://faculty.washington.edu/mlg/courses/definitions/queer.htm

[7] See: http://www-a.ibit.uni-oldenburg.de/bisdoc_redirect/publikationen/bisverlag/unireden/ur97/kap1.pdf

[8] See: http://www.ehow.com/how-does_4811248_surrogate-pregnancy-work.html

[9] See: http://www.fira.ca/cms/documents/168/when_dad_becomes_mom.pdf

References

Abrams, P. (1982) *Historical sociology*, West Compton House: Open Books Publishing Ltd.

Allison, P.D. (1984) *Event history analysis. Regression for longitudinal event data*, London: Sage.

Basow, S.A. (1992) *Gender: stereotypes and roles* (3rd edn), Pacific Grove, CA: Thomson Learning.

Berger, T. and Luckmann, P.L. (1967) *The social construction of reality: A treatise in the sociology of knowledge*, London: Penguin Books.

Boslaugh, S. (2007) *Secondary data sources for public health: a practical guide*, New York, NY: Cambridge University Press.

Brown, G.W. and Moran, P.M. (1997) 'Single mothers, poverty and depression', *Psychological Medicine*, vol 27, pp 21–33.

Comte, A. (1842) *Cours de philosophie positive* (vol I), Paris: A. Costes.

Coupland, D. (1991) *Generation X: Tales for an accelerated culture*, New York: St Martin's Press.

Davies, P. (1992) 'The role of disclosure in coming out among gay men', in K. Plummer (ed) *Modern homosexualities: fragments of lesbian and gay experience*, London: Routledge, pp 75–83.

Elder, G.H., Jr (1985) 'Perspectives on the life course', in G.H. Elder Jr (ed) *Life course dynamics. Trajectories and transitions, 1968–1980*, Ithaca, NY, and London: Cornell University Press, pp 23–49.

Elder, G.H., Jr (1992) 'Life course', in E.F. Borgatta and M.L. Borgatta (eds) *Encyclopedia of sociology* (vol 3), New York, NY: MacMillan, pp 1120–30.

Erbe, B. (2012) 'Will there be a fourth wave feminism?', *The Analyst Journal*, The Egalitarian Press, 23 April. Available at: www.analystjournal.com/component/k2/item/1214-will-there-be-a-fourth-wave-of-feminism?.html

Federal/Provincial/Territorial Status of Women Ministers (2001) 'Women's economic independence and security'. Available at: http://dsp-psd.pwgsc.gc.ca/Collection/SW21-77-2001E.pdf

Foucault, M. (1976–84) *Histoire de la sexualité* (3 vols), Paris: Gallimard.

Fraser, N. and Gordon, L. (1994) '"Dependency" demystified: inscriptions of power in a keyword of the welfare state', *Social Politics*, vol 1, no 1, pp 4–31.

Garfinkel, H., with R.J. Stoller (1967) 'Passing and the managed achievement of sex status in an intersexed person', in H. Garfinkel (ed) *Studies in ethnomethodology*, Englewood Cliffs, NJ: Prentice Hall.

Gerstel, N. and Gross, H. (1982) 'Commuter marriages: a review', *Marriage and Family Review*, vol 5, no 2, pp 71–93.

Giddens, A. (1992) *The transformation of intimacy: sexuality, love, and eroticism in modern societies*, Cambridge: Polity Press.

Gross, M. (2003) *L'homoparentalité*, Paris: Presses Universitaires de France-PUF.

Grusek, J.E. and Hastings, D. (2007) *Handbook of socialization: theory and research*, New York, NY: The Guildford Press.

Haferkamp, H. and Smelser, N.J. (eds) (1992) *Social change and modernity*, Berkeley and Los Angeles, CA: University of California Press.

Heaton, J. (1998) 'Secondary analysis of qualitative data', *Social Research Update 22*. Available at: http://sru.soc.surrey.ac.uk/SRU22.html

Howe, N. and Strauss, W. (1991) *Generations: the history of America's future, 1584 to 2069*, New York, NY: Quill William Morrow.

Hunter, S. (2007) *Coming out and disclosures: LGBT persons across the life span*, New York, NY: Haworth Press.

Katz, C. (2001) 'Vagabond capitalism and the necessity of social reproduction', *Antipode*, vol 33, no 4, pp 709–28.

Kimmel, M.S. (1996) *Manhood in America: A cultural history*, New York: Free Press.

Kirsch, M.H. (2000) *Queer theory and social change*, London and New York, NY: Routledge.

Land, H. (1989) 'The construction of dependency', in M. Bulmer, J. Lewis, and D. Piachaud (eds), *The goals of social policy*, London: Unwin Hyman.

Lister, R. (1990) 'Women, economic dependency and citizenship', *Journal of Social Policy*, vol 19, no 4, pp 445-67.

Lorber, J. (2000) 'Using gender to undo gender: a feminist degendering movement', *Feminist Theory*, vol 1, no 1, pp 79–95.

Lorber, J. (2001) 'The variety of feminisms and their contributions to gender equality', in J. Lorber (ed) *Gender inequality. Feminist theories and politics*, Los Angeles, CA: Roxbury Publishing Company, pp 1–17.

Lorber, J. (2010) *Gender inequality. Feminist theories and politics* (4th edn), New York, NY, and Oxford: Oxford University Press. Available at: http://poliscifi.pbworks.com/f/lorber_feminisms_2010.pdf

Monro, S. (2006) 'Transgender youth: stories of an excluded population', in C. Leccardi and E. Ruspini (eds) *A new youth? Young people, generations and family life*, Aldershot: Ashgate Publishing, pp 298–320.

Orton, J. and Crossman, S. (1988) 'Long Distance Marriage (LDM): cause of marital disruption or a solution to unequal dual-career development?', in D.B. Gutknecht, E.W. Butler, L. Criswell and J. Meints (eds), *Family, self, and society: Emerging issues, alternatives, and interventions*, Lanham, MD: University Press of America, pp 327-46.

Prosser, J. (1998) *Second skins: the body narratives of transsexuality*, New York, NY: Columbia University Press.

Ruspini, E. (2002) *Introduction to longitudinal research*, London and New York, NY: Routledge.

Smelser, N.J. (1981) *Sociology*, Englewood Cliffs, NJ: Prentice Hall.

Smith, E. (2006) *Using secondary data in educational and social research*, Milton Keynes: Open University Press.

Spillman, L. (ed) (2002) *Cultural sociology*, Malden, MA, and London: Blackwell.

Taris, T.W. (2000) *A primer in longitudinal data analysis*, London: Sage Publications.

Uziel, P., Silva da Cunha, C., and Torres I. (2007) 'Homoparentalidade: estratégia política e cotidiano' ('Homoparenthood: Political Strategy and Daily Exercise'), *Omertaa, Journal of Applied Anthropology*, vol 2007/2, pp 118-125, available at: http://www.omertaa.org/archive/omertaa0015.pdf

Van der Kamp, L.J.Th. and Bijleveld, C.C.J.H. (1998) 'Methodological issues in longitudinal research', in C.C.J.H. Bijleveld et al (eds) *Longitudinal data analysis. Designs, models and methods*, London: Sage Publications, pp 1–45.

Woodward, K. (2011) *The short guide to gender*, Bristol: The Policy Press.

Index

Note: Page numbers followed by 'n' refer to footnotes, e.g. 127n. Page numbers followed by 'g' refer to definitions in the glossary, e.g. 143g.